THE SERIALS MANAGEMENT HANDBOOK

A practical guide to print and electronic serials management

Edited by

Tony Kidd and Lyndsay Rees-Jones

LIBRARY ASSOCIATION PUBLISHING
LONDON

Published by
Library Association Publishing
7 Ridgmount Street
London WC1E 7AE

Library Association Publishing is wholly owned by The Library Association.

Published 2000
Reprinted 2001

British Library Cataloguing in Publication Data
A catalogue record for this book is available from the British Library.

ISBN 1-85604-355-X

Typeset in 11/13 Elegant Garamond and Humanist 521 from author's disk by Library Association Publishing.
Printed and made in Great Britain by Antony Rowe Ltd, Chippenham, Wiltshire.

Contents

The contributors

Michael Archer BSc BA MIInfSc   Mick is Principal Information Scientist at AstraZeneca R&D Charnwood. Having originally managed the library service there, his present role is to negotiate global contracts with publishers for access to electronic journals. He moved to his present job after being Information Manager at SmithKline Beecham in Worthing for ten years and at Koch Light Laboratories, Haverhill for the previous eight years. He has a degree in chemistry from Sheffield University and a BA from the Open University specializing in computing and IT. Mick is a member of the UK Serials Group Committee and has been on the editorial board of *Serials* for a number of years. He is a member of the Institute of Information Scientists.

  AstraZeneca R&D Charnwood, Information Science & Library, Bakewell Road, Loughborough, Leicestershire LE11 5RH, UK
  Tel: +44 (0)1509 644235; Fax: +44 (0)1509 645569
  e-mail: michael.archer@astrazeneca.com

Roger Brown BSc ALA   After qualifying as a librarian, Roger Brown spent a brief period in the public library service in the UK before joining the Information Department of Beecham Pharmaceuticals. In 1990 he was appointed Senior Librarian with SmithKline Beecham (SB) with particular responsibilities for library collections and vendor contracts worldwide. Now, as Principal Librarian, Roger specializes in negotiating and licensing information products from vendors, and also in copyright. But as more of SB's library collections become electronically based, the support and development of these electronic resources now take more of his time.

  SmithKline Beecham Pharmaceuticals, Research and Development, Third Avenue, Harlow, Essex CM19 5AW, UK
  Tel: +44 (0) 1279 627317; e-mail: roger_d_brown@sbphrd.com

Tony Kidd MA ALA   Tony Kidd is Head of Serials and Document Delivery at Glasgow University Library, a post he has held since 1991, although Document Delivery was only added to his responsibilities in 1999, in recognition of the growing interdependence between acquisition and access at the article level. He has also worked at Southampton, Aston and Iowa State University Libraries. His particular interests include tendering for serials supply, and the development of electronic journals. He has published in a number of journals, including *Ariadne*, *Learned Publishing*, *Managing Information*, *New Review of Academic Librarianship*, *Serials*, *Serials Librarian*, and *Serials Review*.

Glasgow University Library, Hillhead Street, Glasgow G12 8QE, Scotland, UK
Tel: +44 (0)141 330 6778; Fax: +44 (0) 141 330 4198
e-mail: t.kidd@lib.gla.ac.uk

Jack Meadows MA MSc DPhil DSc FLA FIInfSc FInstP Jack Meadows joined the Department of Information Science at Loughborough University as Professor and Head of Department in 1986. He has subsequently occupied positions as Dean and Pro-Vice-Chancellor. He was previously Professor of Astronomy and the History of Science and Dean at Leicester University. During that time he also headed the Primary Communications Centre and the Office for Humanities Communication.

Professor of Library and Information Studies, Loughborough University, Loughborough, Leicestershire LE11 3TU, UK
Tel: +44 (0) 1509 223082; e-mail: a.j.meadows@lboro.ac.uk

Sally Morris MA BPhil MIMgt Sally Morris has been involved in publishing for nearly 30 years. She became Secretary-General of the Association of Learned and Professional Society Publishers in August 1998; she also works as a freelance publishing and copyright consultant. For the previous three-and-a-half years she was Director of Copyright and Licensing for John Wiley and Sons Ltd. Before that she spent 11 years with Churchill Livingstone, the then medical division of Longman, building up and managing a substantial journals programme. In earlier years she worked in a wide variety of types of publishing. She has degrees in English and medieval studies from Cambridge and York Universities, and is a member of the Institute of Management.

Morris Associates, South House, The Street, Clapham, Worthing, West Sussex BN13 3UU, UK
Tel: +44 (0) 1903 871686; e-mail: sally@morris-assocs.demon.co.uk
http://www.alpsp.org.uk

Albert Prior Albert Prior is Business Development Director at Swets and Zeitlinger, the international subscription agent and information services company. He has held a number of positions in Swets in the more than 20 years that he has been with them, including Managing Director of Swets UK Ltd, International Publisher Relations Manager, Electronic Services, and head of promotion and product development. Prior to joining Swets he worked for Blackwell's in sales and marketing, having originally trained as a librarian. He is past Chair of the United Kingdom Serials Group and former Editor of *Serials*, the Journal of the UKSG. Albert has given presentations at a number of conferences and seminars, on the role of subscription agents and intermediaries in the electronic environment. He is a member of the management board of NESLI, the UK National Electronic Site Licence Initiative, Joint Editor of *Scholarly Communications Report*, the industry newsletter, and an active member of the Association of Subscription Agents.

> Swets and Zeitlinger BV, 32 Blacklands Way, Abingdon Business Park, Abingdon OX14 1SX, UK
> Tel: +44 (0) 1235 530809; Fax: +44 (0) 1235 535055
> e-mail: aprior@swets.co.uk; http://www.swets.nl

Lyndsay Rees-Jones BA ALA FRSA Lyndsay is Professional Adviser, Special Libraries and Information Services at The Library Association. Prior to joining the LA in 1997 she worked in industry, latterly as the Librarian/Information Officer for National Grid plc. Lyndsay's professional interests range from supporting and encouraging the individual in the workplace, to the promotion of effectively managed information to industry and commerce. She is currently keen to identify and connect the large number of professionals working in isolation in the (relatively) hidden world of workplace libraries. Her long-term involvement with the United Kingdom Serials Group, where she has served as Marketing Officer and Secretary, stems from her belief in the strength of a forum which brings together all the participants in the sector.

> The Library Association, 7 Ridgmount Street, London WC1E 7AE, UK
> Tel: +44 (0) 20 7255 0635; e-mail: lyndsay.rees-jones@la-hq.org.uk

Matthew Searle MA DipLib ALA Matthew Searle joined the senior management group of the Radcliffe Science Library, University of Oxford, in 1994, after a number of years working at the University of Birmingham, and has been Technical Services Librarian since creation of the post in 1997. Most of his career has been spent working with periodicals and on two occasions he has been closely involved with the introduction of new library housekeeping systems. He chairs the Serials Special Interest Group in the University of Oxford, and his current professional concern is with the cataloguing of electronic journals. He has written several articles concerning serials, and is also co-compiler of the latest supplement to *Ottley's bibliography of British railway history*.

> Radcliffe Science Library, University of Oxford Parks Road, Oxford OX1 3QP, UK
> Tel: +44 (0) 1865 272819; e-mail: ms@bodley.ox.ac.uk

Liz Stevenson BA DipLib   Liz Stevenson is Serials Librarian at Edinburgh University Library, with experience also in book acquisitions. She has Library-wide responsibility for serials-related strategy, development and training, with particular responsibility for acquisition in the Main Library. Liz is coordinator of the Edinburgh Libraries Federations Union List of Serials, providing coverage of the current serials holdings of academic and research libraries in Edinburgh. This List forms part of SALSER, which lists serials held in Scottish Confederation of University and Research Libraries' (SCURL) collections. Liz was recently involved in a SCURL-wide tender as a member of the SHERAL Serials Tendering Working Group.

Edinburgh University Library, George Square, Edinburgh EH8 9LJ, Scotland, UK

Tel: +44 (0) 131 651 1519; e-mail: l.stevenson@ed.ac.uk

Jill Taylor-Roe BA MA ALA   Jill Taylor-Roe is Sub-Librarian, Liaison and Academic Services at the University of Newcastle upon Tyne, where she leads the team of faculty liaison librarians and manages the Library's acquisitions budget. She read English literature at university and her intention after graduating was to pursue research in 18th century literature and art. However, a year working in the University Library at Newcastle persuaded her of the error of her ways and she subsequently completed an MA in librarianship at Sheffield. Her professional interests include consortia purchasing, the selection and management of journals (both print and electronic) and the integration of information skills training within academic curricula. Jill currently chairs the NEYEL Purchasing Consortium, which comprises twenty two academic libraries in the North, North East, Yorkshire and Midlands of England and is an active member of the United Kingdom Serials Group, serving on both the main Committee and on its education group.

Newcastle University Library, The Robinson Library, University of Newcastle, Newcastle upon Tyne, NE2 4HQ, UK

Tel: +44 (0) 191 222 6000; e-mail: jill.taylor-roe@newcastle.ac.uk

Martin White BSc FIInfSc FRSA   Martin White is Managing Director of Intranet Focus Ltd, which he established in 1999. He has nearly 30 years experience in the information business, in information management, publishing and consulting roles, and has held senior management positions in Reed Publishing, International Data Corporation, Logica, Romtec and TFPL Ltd. His current areas of interest include the management of transnational intranets, the development of enterprise information portals and the future of STM publishing. He is the co-author of the TFPL *Guide to best practice in intranet management* (1998) and the TFPL/Blackwells *Guide to electronic journal management* (1999). Martin is a Past-President of the Institute of Information Scientists, a member of the editorial board of the *International Journal of Information Management*, and a columnist for both *Information World Review* and *Against the Grain*. He has a degree in chemistry from the University of Southampton.

Intranet Focus Ltd, 12 Allcard Close, Horsham, West Sussex RH12 5AJ, UK

Tel. +44 (0) 1403 267030; e-mail: martin.white@intranetfocus.com

http://www.intranetfocus.com

Hazel Woodward PhD BA ALA MIInfSc Hazel has been University Librarian and Director of Cranfield University Press since October 1998. Prior to that she worked at Loughborough University. Hazel's professional interests and research have focused upon scholarly publishing and electronic information issues and she has published widely on these topics and presented papers at many national and international conferences. She has been very active professionally – currently a Committee member (former Chair) of the United Kingdom Serials Group; a member of the SCONUL Committee on Serials and Scholarly Communication; and a member of the JISC NESLI Steering Committee.

Cranfield University, Cranfield, Bedfordshire MK43 0AL, UK

Tel: +44(0)1234 754446; Fax: +44(0)1234 752391

e-mail: h.woodward@cranfield.ac.uk

Introduction

It is now ten years since the last general work on serials management in libraries appeared in the UK (Graham and Buettel, 1990), and seven years since the publication of Woodward and Pilling's *The international serials industry* (1993). Given the ever faster speed of change in this field, the UK Serials Group (UKSG) and Library Association Publishing felt that a new distillation of experience, practice and policies was long overdue. This volume – a collaborative effort by a number of UK librarians and others working in this stimulating and fascinating domain – is the result.

The major change in recent years is of course the advent of the electronic journal, and every chapter in this book reflects that basic development. However, it is still the case that in almost every library, the bulk of day-to-day serials work is concerned with print journals, and the practices and problems arising from dealing with printed issues also feature throughout.

Precisely because of the present pace of change, we have not insisted that our chapter authors provide a comprehensive description of every aspect of current serials management. While authors have been encouraged to concentrate on practical matters, they also consider current developments from a broad policy viewpoint. We hope that this combination will be useful to readers, whether practising serials librarians, students taking library and information courses, or managers in libraries, publishing houses, serials agencies, or in the growing number of intermediaries that are finding new roles to play in the changing serials landscape.

Our contributors work predominantly in UK university libraries, but there are also authors from commercial libraries, and all have striven to range as widely as possible in their analysis, although the majority of examples are drawn from the academic sector. The serials supply chain is of course by no means limited to libraries, although serials management within libraries is the focus of this particular volume. Our introductory chapter, setting the scene with a consideration of the purpose and use of the serial literature, and its development, is written by the prominent historian of the process of scholarly communication, Professor Jack Meadows. There are also chapters covering the world of the journal publisher, a discussion of the work of the serials agent, and a final chapter by Martin White, writing as a consultant with wide experience of all parties in the serials industry.

In a little more detail, following Jack Meadows' erudite defence of the continuing requirement for serial publication, albeit in different formats, Sally Morris of the Association of Learned and Professional Society Publishers (ALPSP) outlines the process of publication, and mounts a spirited defence of the continuing role of the publisher in adding value to the output of researchers, while stressing the need for publishers to adapt to changing technologies and markets. Hazel Woodward and Mick Archer, representing both academic and commercial libraries, look at some of the same issues from the point of view of the serials librarian and library user, discussing the variety of delivery mechanisms now available for the information contained within journal articles.

Proceeding to some of the slightly more down-to-earth practicalities of life as a serials manager, Jill Taylor-Roe examines the processes involved in trying to increase, or more likely to minimize the decrease, of the annual budget for serials, considers some of the factors influencing journal prices, and details management information required to manage the budget. Albert Prior, well-known subscription agent, and Tony Kidd, one of the editors of this volume, then discuss the actual acquisition of the journal, whether physical acquisition of print issues, or access to the electronic equivalent, from the point of view of both the subscription agent and of the librarian. In the next chapter, Matthew Searle writes on processing issues, from claiming to cataloguing, considering their purpose, and underlining the importance of integration of data to provide the most effective service to users.

Moving on, the concept of stock management is covered by Liz Stevenson, reviewing topics ranging from disposal to binding to the currently hotly-debated issue of archiving. Roger Brown brings his experience of commercial information services to his contribution on exploitation and usage analysis, including influence on cancellation policies and differences in measurement for print and electronic journals. Finally, Martin White sums up some of the threats and opportunities open to the different partners in this supply chain – authors, publishers, database providers, subscription agents, and librarians.

From the foregoing very brief summaries, the reader will see that there is potential for overlap between chapter content. We as editors have been aware of this and controlled it to some extent, but have not attempted complete demarcation, both because this would cause artificial restrictions, and, more importantly, limit different viewpoints and emphases put forward by different authors. It is unlikely that there has ever been one 'right' view, procedure, or solution in this subject, and this is certainly true at the present time, when the future of scholarly communication is unclear to all, even perhaps to the most passionate advocates of one outcome or another.

Most books on serials start with a definition of the term 'serial', perhaps distinguishing it from related terms such as 'periodical' and 'journal'. Although Jack Meadows gives some examples of 'serials' in his introductory chapter, we as editors have not felt this to be an issue of great debate in this country. This does on occasion cause problems, for example over deciding on the exact size of serials business among different partners in a consortium, or contributing comparable figures to national statistics, but it is very unlikely that there will ever be complete consistency in practice between serials departments over the country as a whole. To help reach a reasonable consensus, the definition given in the second edition 1998 revision of the *Anglo-American cataloguing rules (AACR2)* is as useful as any. There, a serial is defined as 'a publication in any medium issued in successive parts bearing numeric or chronological designations and intended to be continued indefinitely. Serials include periodicals; newspapers; annuals (reports, yearbooks, etc); the journals, memoirs, proceedings, transactions, etc, of societies; and numbered monographic series' (AACR2, 1998).

This book has in the main highlighted the coverage of practice in the UK, although of course serials originate from and are distributed to all parts of the world, and there are many references to relevant developments elsewhere, especially given the international nature of the electronic journal, and the ability of the world wide web and the Internet to abolish national frontiers, together with the multinational reach of many relevant companies and organizations. We should note that American serials practice has been well covered in recent books by, for example, Marcia Tuttle (1996), Thomas Nisonger (1998), Jean Walter Farrington (1997) and Dora Chen Chiou-Sen (1995). These books all have different emphases, from each other and from this volume, and are all worth examining. Although their focus is North American, the worldwide serials interconnections mean that they contain many relevant insights. The International Federation of Library Associations and Institutions (IFLA) has also published a relatively recent guide, aimed at serials librarians throughout the world, particularly in developing countries (Szilvassy, 1996).

Although there have been no very recent UK published books covering serials management for librarians in general, the administration of electronic journals has been discussed in, for example, *TFPL/Blackwell's guide to electronic journal management* (1999). Other large subscription agents are often useful sources of information in this area as well, for example Harrassowitz's *Electronic journals: a selected resource guide* (1999) gives a valuable overview. Guides to relevant websites are provided by *Serials in cyberspace*, maintained by Birdie MacLennan of the University of Vermont Libraries; and by Ann Ercelawn's *Tools for serials catalogers*. The websites of the UKSG and NASIG, mentioned below, are also very useful in this respect.

We have not attempted to include a comprehensive bibliography, although each chapter includes references to some relevant articles, as well as, usually, pointers to useful websites. Some of the US works cited in the previous paragraphs (eg Nisonger) have lengthy bibliographies. A very useful source is the *Scholarly electronic publishing bibliography*, compiled and issued regularly on the web by Charles Bailey via the University of Houston Libraries, although restricted as the title implies to works, and websites, relevant to electronic publishing. *Index Morganagus* and *Current cites* are other helpful listings of articles relevant to serials, while, more generally, the BUBL Journals service performs an important current awareness task for relevant journals literature, and *Library and information service abstracts* (*LISA*) (and *Library literature & information science* in the USA) provide a comprehensive service.

One of the best sources for information on electronic journals is *NewJour*, which provides indexed daily updates of new journals and newsletters available on the Internet. The *ARL directory of electronic journals, newsletters and academic discussion lists* is also useful, although the most recent, seventh, edition was published in early 1998, a long time ago in this fast-changing world. The well-established titles such as *Ulrich's international periodicals directory* or the *Serials directory* cover electronic and print journals, and once again the serials agents produce very thorough print and electronic serials listings.

The references at the ends of chapters will give the reader an idea of where relevant articles on serials management are to be found, but a brief overview may be helpful here, with apologies to the many useful sources not listed. In the UK, the UKSG journal *Serials* has become indispensable, while ALPSP's *Learned publishing* also contains very many significant articles. The American *Serials librarian* and *Serials review* are also important. A recent new entry in the field is *Library consortium management*, launched in 1999. Journals with a slightly more tangential interest for serials include, in the UK, *Vine* (covering library systems), *Program*, and *The electronic library*, and, in the US, *Library collections, acquisitions, and technical services* (formerly *Library acquisitions: practice and theory*), *Library resources and technical services*, and *Against the grain*. Electronic journals are now an important resource, and those interested should regularly consult such titles as *Ariadne*, *D-Lib magazine*, *First Monday*, and *Journal of electronic publishing*. The *Newsletter on serials pricing issues* (*NSPI*), founded and maintained by Marcia Tuttle, is a particularly useful source of up-to-date information and debate.

Mention of *NSPI*, not a traditional journal but more of a forum for discussion, brings us on to the question of discussion lists, certainly more relevant on a day-to-day basis for practitioners, and vital for maintaining an understanding of developments, and a feel for the fervent debates taking place on 'the future' and how to approach it. American lists tend to have more contributions, perhaps because there are more US librarians, but relevant British lists include *lis-serials*, *lis-e-journals* (recently set up by the UKSG to cater for specific problems with and discussion on electronic journals), and *e-collections* (another new list considering databases and licences). In the United States, Birdie MacLennan's *serialst* is the place to discuss practical serials problems, while LIBLICENSE-L (spun off from Ann Okerson's key *LIBLICENSE* website) tends to debate policy questions, particularly with reference to the ubiquitous licensing issues.

In addition to journals and discussion lists, membership of, and contribution to, professional organizations provide an essential means of keeping abreast of significant changes, and an opportunity to network and exchange experience with fellow professionals, through publications, annual conferences and more specialist seminars. While both the Library Association and the American Library Association play important roles here, the nature of the serials supply chain has led to the establishment of separate organizations, incorporating all the players – librarians, publishers, agents and other intermediaries – within the industry. The UK Serials Group was set up informally in 1978, but has developed into an organization of 600 institutional members, from all sectors and many different countries (Harwood, 1999). Its annual Spring conference with a regular attendance of around 500 has become the most important event of the year for many in the serials world in the UK and other European countries, both for the quality of the papers presented and, perhaps more importantly, for the chance to mix, talk, negotiate, and do business with others present. The North American Serials Interest Group (NASIG) followed the UKSG in 1985, also holding an annual conference, providing the *NASIG newsletter* to members, and mounting, like UKSG, an important website with information and many helpful links. There are also serials groups operating in other European countries, including the Netherlands, Germany, and Scandinavian nations; and elsewhere, such as the Australian Serials Special Interest Group (ASSIG).

We hope that this volume will be both useful and interesting to all those working with serials, and to those who would like to know a little more about developments which are already revolutionizing the nature of scholarly communication. Above all, whilst we have endeavoured to deliver an accessible and useful insight into the serials world as it is today, this is a field of communication that has transformed itself dramatically in recent years, and will continue to do so for many years to come. We anticipate that the reader will interpret and develop the text. Each situation, or combination of situations, is unique; so by being open-minded and flexible, by altering and adapting, what follows will stimulate development and add to the collective understanding of the role of serials.

Acknowledgments

The Editors would like to acknowledge that without the help of a large number of people this book would not have reached you. Our eternal thanks to the authors, who not only accepted our invitation to contribute, but also coped valiantly with our novice editing style. The book is truly theirs.

Thanks also to Helen Carley, Beth Barber, Lin Franklin and colleagues at LA Publishing, whose patience makes the thought of editing another book almost attractive. And to our busy and professional colleagues on the UKSG Committee who made time to comment and advise.

And finally we thank our families; Sue, Helen and Alastair, Robin, Rhiannon and Angharad for their support, the endless cups of tea and for still being our families.

References

Against the grain, College of Charleston, SC.

Anglo-American cataloguing rules (1998) 2nd edn 1998 revision, Library Association Publishing, 622.

Ariadne
   http://www.ariadne.ac.uk/

Australian Serials Special Interest Group (ASSIG)
   http://www.alia.org.au/sigs/assig/

BUBL Journals
   http://www.bubl.ac.uk/journals/

Chiou-Sen, D C (1995) *Serials management: a practical guide*, American Library Association.

Current cites: an annotated bibliography of selected articles, books, and digital documents on information technology, available at:
   http://sunsite.berkeley.edu/CurrentCites/

D-Lib magazine
   http://mirrored.ukoln.ac.uk/lis-journals/dlib/dlib/dlib.html

e-collections
   http://www.mailbase.ac.uk/lists/e-collections/

The electronic library, Learned Information Europe Ltd.

Farrington, J W (1997) *Serials management in academic libraries: a guide to issues and practices*, Greenwood Press.

First Monday
   http://www.firstmonday.dk/

Graham, M and Buettel, F (eds) (1990) *Serials management: a practical guide*, Aslib.

Harrassowitz (1999) *Electronic journals: a selected resource guide*, available at:

http://www.harrassowitz.de/ms/ejresguide.html

Harwood, P (1999) *The serials community: an eternal triangle seeks collaboration through dialogue*, Logos, **10** (2), 81–2.

Index Morganagus: a full-text index of library-related electronic serials
http://sunsite.berkeley.edu/IndexMorganagus/

Journal of electronic publishing
http://www.press.umich.edu/jep/

Learned publishing, Association of Learned and Professional Society Publishers.

LIBLICENSE
http://www.library.yale.edu/~llicense/index.shtml

LIBLICENSE-L
http://www.library.yale.edu/~llicense/mailing-list.shtml

Library and information science abstracts, Bowker-Saur.

Library collections, acquisitions and technical services, Pergamon.

Library consortium management, MCB.

Library literature & information science, H W Wilson.

Library resources and technical services, American Library Association, Association for Library Collections and Technical Services.

lis-e-journals
http://www.mailbase.ac.uk/lists/lis-e-journals/

lis-serials
http://www.mailbase.ac.uk/lists/lis-serials/

NewJour: electronic journals and newsletters
http://gort.ucsd.edu/newjour/

Newsletter on serials pricing issues
http://www-mathdoc.ujf-grenoble.fr/NSPI/NSPIe.html

Nisonger, T E (1998) *Management of serials in libraries*, Libraries Unlimited.

North American Serials Interest Group Inc (NASIG)
http://www.nasig.org/

Program, Aslib.

Scholarly Electronic Publishing Bibliography
http://info.lib.uh.edu/sepb/sepb.html

Serials, UK Serials Group.

Serials directory, EBSCO.

Serials in cyberspace: collections, resources and services
http://www.uvm.edu/~bmaclenn/

The serials librarian, Haworth Information Press.

Serials review, Elsevier.

serialst
http://www.uvm.edu/~bmaclenn/serialst.html

Szilvassy, J (1996) *Basic serials management handbook*, rev edn, Saur for the IFLA
    Section on Serial Publications.
TFPL/Blackwell's guide to electronic journal management (1999), TFPL.
Tools for serials catalogers
    http://www.library.vanderbilt.edu/ercelawn/serials.html
Tuttle, M (1996) *Managing serials*, JAI Press.
UK Serials Group
    http://www.uksg.org/
Ulrich's international periodicals directory, Bowker-Saur.
Vine, Library Information Technology Centre, South Bank University.
Woodward, H and Pilling, S (eds) (1993) *The international serials industry*, Gower.

1

Why do we need serials?

Jack Meadows

Introduction

The end of the 20th century marks a turning point for serials publication. The keenly debated question is – how will the balance between paper-based and electronic serials change over the next few years? Trying to find an answer to this question entails first understanding why the traditional paper-based system works as it does. This is where we will start.

Serials come in various guises. Those encountered most frequently by a wide range of librarians are contained in a sub-group, usually labelled 'scholarly [or research] journals'. This category will form the main focus of discussion here, though with some side-glances at other categories, such as magazines and monograph series. Two questions need to be answered immediately. First, why do scholars need to communicate via formal channels? (Until recently, 'formal' channels meant almost exclusively print on paper: now it increasingly includes electronic media.) Secondly, why have journals long been accepted as a crucially important way of communicating scholarly work?

Why are there scholarly journals?

Anyone who claims to be communicating research must be trying to say something original about the world in which we live. The newness may lie either in the observations, or in ideas about how such observations should be interpreted. Such content is a necessary condition for a journal to be scholarly, but it is hardly sufficient. After all, other categories of serials – newspapers, for example – might be said to do the same. The difference is that the material in a scholarly journal is expected to be based on the application of appropriate research methods. These vary from subject to subject, but always need to be acceptable to the research community involved.

This explains, in a rather summary way, what is meant by 'scholarly' in the term 'scholarly journal'. It does not explain why a formal channel, such as a journal, is considered necessary for the communication of research information. The reason is that all research is, to a greater or lesser extent, a cumulative process. If I decide to plan a new research project today, my plans will depend, in part, on what relevant research on the topic has been done previously. The importance of previous work will vary from subject to subject. New research in literary theory, for example, is likely to be less dependent on previous work than new research in chemistry. But, as PhD students in any subject will gloomily admit, one of the inescapable acts of a researcher's life is the literature search. Such a search means that I must have access to past research. This implies, in turn, that the previous research must have been recorded in such a way that it is still available for consultation. Long-term storage of information – sometimes optimistically labelled 'permanent' storage – is what defines a formal mode of communication.

As with any form of publication, journals have an input and an output end. When I am carrying out a literature search, I am at the output end, and expect to find the research I need recorded in a durable form. I use this information to produce a new piece of research. When it is finished, I move to the input end. I want to tell my colleagues what I have found. Since I am attached to my results, I want them to reach not only today's audience, but others yet to come unto the third or fourth generation. In other words, if I consider my results worthwhile, I want them to be on 'permanent' record. More than that, unless I try to make my results available on a long-term basis, my colleagues will assume that they are not very important. So both at the input and output ends of research, participants wish to access a formal channel.

This still does not answer the question – why journals? After all, much scholarly research is happily communicated via books. One might put this in a different way: if journals did not exist, would it be necessary to invent them? Though the topic of interest may be wide-ranging, researchers typically have to cut it down into smaller segments in order to investigate it in depth. One way forward is to wait until all these segments have been examined, then to put the results together and publish them as a lengthy thesis. In many subjects, the time delay involved may be dangerous: researchers may find that their work is pre-empted by a colleague who publishes first. Even with a subject such as history, where lengthy publication of research in book form is common, some facets of the research may be valuable in themselves, though not suitable for inclusion in the book. The overall result is that in all fields of research there is a need to publish short contributions.

The economics of print publishing are such that it rarely makes sense to produce and distribute small specialist pamphlets. It is a much more viable proposition to bundle together several short contributions dealing with the same specialist topic, and sell them as a single publication. Authors typically want reasonably rapid publication to prevent their material from going out-of-date. Similarly, readers, particularly where they are researchers themselves, want up-to-date information. Hence, such bundling of separate items for publication needs to be done at fairly frequent intervals (as compared with the publication delay time for book publication). Lo and behold – we have reinvented the scholarly journal. So, in the world of print, there are good economic and research reasons why scholarly journals should exist. Some of this logic applies to serials other than scholarly journals. For example, newspapers consist of a number of smaller items, which it would not be feasible to publish separately, brought together in a single publication. Newspapers, too, must be produced rapidly in order not to be preempted, in this case predominantly by competing newspapers.

The early days of serials

The nature of newspapers is actually relevant to the origins of the scholarly journal. Prior to the 1660s, news of research was normally transmitted either via books or letters. The latter were not usually meant to be private correspondence in the way that most present-day letters are. Rather they conveyed information on work carried out by the writers and their friends to be communicated by the recipients to their own circles of friends and acquaintances. Using letters obviously had its limitations. The audiences for them were restricted in size, and the medium employed could hardly be called permanent. During the first half of the 17th century, newspapers became an increasingly acceptable way for disseminating news. It is hardly surprising that the idea should have occurred of putting together letters, and publishing them in the same way as the different news items in a newspaper. This led in the 1660s to the appearance of the first two journals that can be classified as 'scholarly' in the modern sense, *Philosophical Transactions* in England and *Journal des Sçavans* in France (Manten, 1980). It is an interesting exercise to scan early and more recent copies of *Philosophical Transactions*, and to see how the early letters, reproduced in the form they were received, have gradually transmuted in their layout into the modern journal article.

The fact that letters circulated between groups of people was significant in deciding who published the new journals. Such groups frequently coalesced into societies. These were organized on a formal basis, and typically undertook the publication of journals as a part of their activities. Such institutionalization provided some stability for the process of journal publication. Societies have usually had a more extended lifetime than less formal groupings, as can be seen from a scan of the lengthy journal backruns possessed by many academic and national libraries. Because the journals were primarily intended for members, their cost was normally offset against members' subscriptions. Apart from members' copies, a society's journals were often used as barter to exchange for copies of journals published by other societies. In this way, a society's library could provide reasonable coverage of the field with little actual expenditure. One consequence of this limited circulation was that the question of pricing societies' journals was seldom seen as pressing. Societies could also produce serial publications other than journals. For example, monograph series were often particularly important for societies dealing with observational sciences (such as geology), or topics in the humanities. An example from the latter field is the Early English Text Society, which was set up in the 1860s specifically to produce a series of scholarly editions of old English literature.

Non-society publishers, more especially university presses, also had an early interest in the production of monograph series. They were less active in terms of journal publication up to the 20th century. It was not that they made no attempt to publish journals: rather, commercially produced journals often proved to be financially unviable. Consequently, those commercially published journals that did appear tended to have short lifetimes (Brock, 1980). There were exceptions. The *Philosophical Magazine*, which first appeared toward the end of the 18th century, is still with us, as is *Nature*, which was launched at the end of the 1860s. However, the latter title points up the problem for commercial publishers: it was over 30 years after the launch of *Nature* before its publisher, Macmillan, started making a profit on it. The problem until the 20th century was the limited size of the audience for specialized publications.

The growth of serials

The 19th century saw a growth in the size of a literate middle class throughout Western Europe and North America. The result was a demand for more general reading matter, including more by the way of serial literature. In consequence, it became increasingly feasible to publish magazines and journals aimed at an educated audience. In Britain, for example, starting with the *Edinburgh Review* (established in 1802), a wide range of general periodicals was created during the 19th century. Even so, subscriptions were quite low – a few thousand – so their financial position could sometimes be precarious. Even more specialized publications could survive, if the material was presented for a general audience. An example is the *Scientific American*, which first appeared in 1845.

In the 20th century, readers have experienced continuing growth both in their disposable income and in the amount of leisure time available. The market for serials has therefore increased greatly. Beginning with newspapers and then extending to magazines, the overall circulation of serials aimed at a general audience expanded throughout the first half of the 20th century. For specialist journals, the market remained restricted during this period, and society publications continued to dominate. World War 2 acted as a catalyst for change. The scientific and technological advances triggered by the war – most obviously, the atomic bomb – ensured that post-war governments saw an urgent need to pump more funds into research and development work, and, consequently, into the training of specialists. Though this support was aimed primarily at scientists and engineers, the growth in universities stimulated an increase in student, and therefore staff, population across faculties. The result was a rapid increase both in the number of people interested in publishing original work and in the audience for such writing. The learned and professional societies experienced some difficulty in coping with this new situation. The first societies often had quite wide interests, and this was reflected in the contents of the journals they published. As time passed, researchers' interests became more and more specialized. They were catered for by the creation of more specialist societies producing more specialized journals. However, such fragmentation occurred at a relatively leisurely pace. In the period of rapid change after World War 2, the need for specialist knowledge became increasingly emphasized. Commercial publishers, with their greater flexibility, were better able to step into this gap quickly than were society publishers.

The problem of cost

Adverse comments on the cost of journal subscriptions are nothing new. In the latter part of the 19th century, when Germany became the most influential country in the academic world, commercial publishers in Germany – notably Springer – began to produce journals. By the early years of the 20th century, grumbles about the prices of some of these journals could already be heard (Meadows, 1993). But the question of journal pricing became much more central after World War 2. One step that caused much debate was the introduction of differential pricing for individuals and institutions, with the latter paying considerably more. (The inspiration seems to have come from Robert Maxwell's newly founded Pergamon Press.) This soon became common practice. Many societies initially continued to package their journals as part of members' subscriptions, but paid more attention to external sales. It then became apparent that a significant number of members no longer wished to continue receiving the journal if this meant large increases in members' subscriptions. In consequence, a two-tier system, with a smaller subscription for members who did not take journals, came to be adopted by many societies.

Complaints by librarians about the growing cost of journal subscriptions have increased from the 1960s onwards. Subscription prices have grown by a few hundred per cent from one decade to the next. Some of the increase can be attributed to inflation, and some to the growing size of many journals (Moline, 1989). In terms of price increases, society publishers have moved closer to commercial publishers. They have recognized that journals can be a major source of income on which they should capitalize. The scale of the increases has varied – for example, with subject. Subscriptions have increased much more rapidly for science journals than for journals in the humanities. An important issue here is the market: scientific journals have come to rely primarily on institutional purchase, whereas some humanities journals still hope for significant purchases by individuals. This varies with country: for example, individual purchasing of journals is commoner in the USA than the UK. One aspect widely noted has been that price increases for commercial journals have been consistently larger than for society journals. Commercial publishers have explained the difference in terms of the hidden subsidies enjoyed by society publishers (eg in terms of unpaid editorial work). Librarians have tended to be suspicious of this argument.

The basic difficulty with all these price increases is that they have exceeded the growth in purchasing power not only of many individuals, but even of many institutions. For example, major research libraries in the USA had increases in their acquisitions budgets during the 1970s and 1980s which appreciably exceeded the rate of inflation. The proportion of their budgets which they devoted to the purchase of serials rose from 40% to over 55% over this period. Yet their average serials holdings dropped from about a third of the relevant titles to just over a quarter (Page, Campbell and Meadows, 1997, 20–1). A typical library policy for many years past has been that acquisition of a new journal title must be balanced by cancellation of an equivalent title. Since new journal titles have continued to be launched, the overall result has been for the circulation of many existing journals to fall. In order to maintain their income, journal publishers usually either increase the prices of their existing journals, or launch new ones. The drawback is that this response simply adds to the existing problem. The increasingly urgent question has therefore been how to break out of this vicious circle.

Acquisition problems thus relate in part to the continuing appearance of new journal titles. For much of the 20th century, there has been a continuing growth in the audience interested in specialist topics. As new specialisms have arisen, so publishers have rushed to provide suitable journals, in the knowledge that there will be a growing audience for them. The journals catering for the old specialisms continue to have an audience, and therefore continue in existence. The result has been that the number of journal titles available has grown rapidly – perhaps by a factor approaching ten between the mid-20th century and its end (Meadows, 1993). In the latter decades of the 20th century, the growth in the number of specialist readers has begun to slow down, mainly owing to financial limitations. Correspondingly, though new journal titles continue to appear, it is at a reduced rate relative to (say) the 1960s (Page, Campbell and Meadows, 1997, 13–14). The position with regard to other serials is rather different. Magazines have also had to adapt to changes in specialist audiences, as the rapid rise of computer magazines bears witness. In this case, a highly competitive market based on purchases by individuals has ensured that both the numbers of titles and their prices have kept within reasonable bounds. Monographic series, though often purchased by the institutional market and increasing in number with time, have seen prices rise at an appreciably slower rate than for journals. Consequently, the serials pricing and proliferation problem is an issue that particularly affects journals.

Accessing serials

Two questions are raised by this proliferation of journals. The first relates to retrieval. Obviously, the more journals there are, the more difficult it is to track down relevant articles. So how can readers be helped to find the information they require? The answer, dating back to the 19th century, has been to provide specialist abstracts journals supplemented by a variety of indexes. Until relatively recently, these have been paper-based guides to paper-based literature. The second question concerns selection. How do readers, authors or librarians decide which are the important journals in a given field? For the most part, assessment of journal ranking has been by word of mouth circulating in the relevant community. Such assessment is not entirely subjective. The journals nominated invariably include high-quality material often written by well-known names in the field. Gut feelings about journals can be supplemented by more quantitative methods. The 'impact factor', based on citation analysis, is frequently mentioned as an aid here. A journal's impact factor for a given period is the number of citations to the journal divided by the number of citable items published. In other words, it is an estimate of how many citations, on average, an article published in that journal receives. The citation data are obtained from the citation indexes published by the Institute of Scientific Information (ISI). The rankings that these impact factors produce within each specialism agree reasonably well with qualitative assessments.

Ensuring quality

If readers and authors are attracted to high-quality publications, this implies two things: first, that there must be some degree of agreement on what constitutes 'high quality', and, secondly, that some mechanism must exist for controlling the quality of what is accepted for publication. From the serials management viewpoint, the most important comment on the first point is that the level of agreement on quality tends to depend on the field. The simplest way of judging quality is to give the material to several experts in the relevant field and to ask their opinions of it. The results from this kind of exercise have to be treated with caution. For example, the assessors have different backgrounds and interests, so they tend to emphasize different characteristics of any manuscript they read. Despite this, it is clear that agreement concerning quality is typically easier in the sciences than in other fields (Zuckerman and Merton, 1971). What this means in practice is that ranking journals in terms of prestige (and so in terms of their desirability for readers) is usually easier and more consistent in the sciences.

In the normal mechanism for assessing quality such expert assessors are usually labelled 'referees' or 'reviewers'. In the world of research, it is the refereed journals that command most respect and prestige. Incoming manuscripts for all journals are initially scanned by the editor. A number of submissions fall at this stage, because, for example, they are not in the appropriate field. In a refereed journal, the remainder are sent out for review. Most journals use two or three referees for each manuscript, in order to obtain a range of opinion. Very good and very bad material can usually be identified readily, but most submissions lie somewhere in the middle. For these, referees typically require the authors to alter or extend their work before it can be accepted. This obviously delays publication, which can set up a conflict for authors and readers. They want the confirmation of quality that a refereeing system provides, but they do not appreciate the delays in publication that result. One way round this is to have journals which can publish brief communications of high quality rapidly. Journals in this category – such as *Nature* and *Science* – tend, hardly surprisingly, to top the impact factor ratings.

Publishing humanities research

Whereas journals are easily the most important channel for publishing new work in the sciences, this is less true of the social sciences, and often not true at all of the humanities. In these latter, authors see books as an important outlet. Part of the reason is that their work is planned on a larger scale, and part is that the space available in humanities journals is relatively small due to the limited finance available. Monograph series generate their own prestige in the same way as journals, though with a greater emphasis on who edits and who publishes the volumes. As compared with the submission of material to journals, there are two major differences. The first is that contributions are usually invited, so that both the author and the topic are specified prior to the actual submission of material. The second is that each monograph has to be assessed for its likely financial contribution to the series.

Electronic serials

This is an outline of the position for printed serials. What then of serials in electronic form? A transition from one medium to another throws the question of how best to communicate back into the melting pot. The preceding sections have traced how the requirements of the scholarly community have affected the production of their work in printed form. These requirements change only slowly with time. A move to a new medium of communication must therefore examine how best to handle the old requirements in the new medium.

The easiest way of discussing this is to backtrack to the reasons for the development of scholarly journals, and see how they apply in the new context. We can start with the need that both authors and readers feel for new work to be reported via formal channels. The distinction between formal and informal channels has arisen, in part, from the nature of print. The difference between a printed journal and a telephone conversation seems too obvious to require discussion. But this distinction is less clear-cut in the electronic world. At first sight, if I send an electronic mail message to a colleague, it seems obvious that I am communicating informally. Yet, with little change, I can use the same channel to distribute my message to many thousand recipients. I can also archive it on my website, so that it will continue to be available in the future. This way of handling the message sounds very similar to formal communication as it has been traditionally understood in the world of print.

Long-term accessibility of electronic data

If the old distinction between formal and informal channels is less useful for electronic communication, we must look again at the preference for publishing via formal channels. The importance of such channels was that they ensured information was preserved and made available over a lengthy period of time. How do the long-term storage properties of electronic media match this requirement? This actually entails asking two questions. The first relates to the intrinsic properties of the specific storage medium. How long will information survive on (say) a CD-ROM before it becomes significantly degraded? The second concerns the currency of the storage facilities. For how long will new hardware and software be able to handle 'old' forms of information before the stored information and the equipment become incompatible? The current answers to these questions are, respectively, 'Don't know' and 'Not too long'. The latter answer is particularly important. If information is to be available in the longer term, it must migrate from obsolete hardware and software to new at intervals. Transferring the information costs money, both directly and in terms of the staff time involved. It has been estimated, indeed, that a library of electronic texts may well be more expensive to maintain than a library of the same texts in printed form, even allowing for the differences in space requirements and retrieval time (Helal and Weiss, 1996).

Costs

Finance is a question that affects the provision of electronic information, as well as its storage. Most network users assume that an electronic journal should cost less than a printed journal. They base this view on the ease with which they, themselves, can prepare and distribute information electronically. Publishers, on the contrary, emphasize that most of the costs of a journal relate to editing it and preparing it for publication. Hence, they claim that large reductions in cost cannot be expected (Russon and Campbell, 1996). The two viewpoints are not totally irreconcilable, since they depend on the scale of the operations involved. The publishers' comments carry weight for a large, high-prestige journal. A small specialist journal, produced with a large input of voluntary effort, should be cheaper to produce in electronic form.

The format: similar or different?

There is a more fundamental question here. Journals appeared because printing and distributing individual articles was not feasible. Is this still true in an electronic environment? After all, it takes little extra effort online to circulate a series of articles separately than together: so why stick to the idea of a regularly appearing 'issue' for an electronic journal? One important obstacle is the financial uncertainty involved. An issue of a journal may contain only one or two articles of interest to a reader, yet the subscription covers all the articles published. If articles could be accessed separately, it would soon become apparent that some articles have only a limited number of readers. So how should individual articles be priced in order to maintain the overall financial viability of the publishing operation? There are additional complications in practice. For example, most users of journals expect to scan an article before deciding to read it in detail. How can this be arranged for separately purchased articles?

There is, of course, a further question. Why have distinct journals? An electronic database can readily handle large numbers of different journals as though they are one. The answer relates partly to the structure of the present publishing system. The economics of print publishing are reasonably well understood: what will happen during a period of transition to electronic publishing is not. Publishers have considerable resources tied up in their journals. Hardly surprisingly, they are moving into electronic publication cautiously. What this means is that most electronic scholarly journals now available are produced as versions of the printed journal, which continues to be published in parallel. It makes obvious sense for publishers to follow similar forms of provision and subscription for the two kinds of journal.

Another part of the answer relates to the needs of authors and readers. They know their way around current journals: where to send a particular article for publication, or where to go in order to read research of a specific type. So, at present, they mostly prefer the electronic version to stick fairly closely to the printed journal in terms both of appearance and of composition. The significant proviso is 'at present'. Authors and readers recognize that greater use should ultimately be made of all the flexibility that electronic handling offers. But they see good reasons for not moving too fast. For example, most people rate reading from a computer screen as less enjoyable than reading from a printed page. Consequently, much reading currently is done from computer printouts, and it is obviously helpful to maintain the traditional journal format for these. Roughly speaking, half of journal reading consists of browsing and half of directed searching (see eg King, McDonald and Roderer, 1981, 165). As with detailed reading, many people find browsing from the screen less easy than from the printed page. Searching, on the contrary, is best done via the electronic version. What is happening, therefore, is that readers are increasingly using whichever version of the journal better suits their immediate needs.

The future of electronic serials

Ultimately, the success or otherwise of electronic journals depends on the attitude of authors. No input of material: no journals. The uncertainty of long-term electronic storage is a deterrent. More important is the prestige of electronic journals. New journals, whether printed or electronic, typically have low prestige at the start, and build up their reputations with time. Electronic journals start with the additional disadvantage of a new medium. Prestige depends on the quality of the material published by the journal. Most authors and readers say they believe that high quality depends on the application of stringent refereeing procedures. Consequently, electronic journals must show themselves to be as carefully vetted as printed journals. The flexibility offered by electronic handling means that a range of approaches to refereeing are possible. However, in order to reassure authors and readers that electronic journals control the quality of their contents just as well as printed journals, traditional refereeing procedures are still the norm. Even so, purely electronic journals face an uphill climb in establishing themselves as high-prestige publications. This is another reason why publication of electronic versions of existing print journals seems a good option for the immediate future.

In terms of audience outreach, the position is less clear. Where the main audience forms a cohesive community with easy access to networked computers, electronic journals offer an attractive alternative to print. But some fields – for example, in the humanities – have scattered audiences with differing levels of access to computer facilities. For such fields, electronic publication may limit the audience outreach. At the same time, if electronic journals prove to be cheaper to publish than printed journals, this could advantage the humanities particularly, leading to a preference for electronic communication.

Where electronic journals should, in principle, do better than print journals is in speed of dissemination. Fields where rapid publication is important are therefore likely to favour electronic communication. Such fields have typically used preprints extensively. These were originally copies of articles awaiting publication, which the authors circulated to colleagues to speed up dissemination. With time, the articles came to be circulated prior to the refereeing process, or even prior to submission to a journal. In recent years, a centralized database of electronic preprints has been set up for high-energy physics, and has since extended to other research fields (Ginsparg, 1998). This unrefereed material is being extensively used and quoted by readers, to the extent that the original article may never actually be submitted to a journal for publication. In the trade-off between speed of publication and stringent refereeing, the former factor has won out. Correspondingly, these electronic preprints have acquired considerable prestige.

It is not only speed of publication that can incline authors and readers towards electronic communication. Another influential factor is the great ability of electronic media to store large quantities of data from which specific items can be retrieved quickly. An obvious example of this is the large quantities of data from satellites received, stored and sorted every day. The human genome programme is an interesting example of how this can impinge on journal publishing. The genetic sequences derived in early days were published in traditional print journals. As techniques improved and the number of researchers increased rapidly, these journals no longer had sufficient space to print all the sequences that were being identified. Even if there had been space, rapid retrieval of specific sequences would have been difficult. The answer – not only for human data, but that for all organisms – has been to develop centralized electronic databanks, to which new sequences can be sent, and from which data on known sequences can be retrieved (Cameron, 1998).

Electronic communication and research communities

Electronic preprints and the human genome databank share an important characteristic: they can be easily and directly accessed by the research community. Printed preprints were distributed to people known by the author. Electronic preprints can be consulted freely by anyone who has a networked computer. In a similar way, genetic sequences printed in journals were available to subscribers: the electronic databank is available to all researchers working in the field. The result is that a much wider community can access these resources than was possible in the days of print. It was commonplace then to talk of 'invisible colleges' – groups of influential researchers who exchanged information between themselves. Electronic communication speeds up the interaction within such groups, but it also typically extends their size and scope. Consequently, it becomes easier for newcomers to participate. The proviso, of course, is that all the participants must possess up-to-date hardware and software together with free access to electronic networks. The requirement of free access, in particular, may prove difficult to maintain in the future, since charging mechanisms are likely to increase in scope.

Since the advent of electronic media is affecting group communication, it might be expected that learned and professional societies would be taking an especial interest in them. Societies have, indeed, done much pioneering work on electronic journals, but their interest has begun to range wider. Society functions typically extend beyond the publication of refereed journals: many societies also provide newsletters, members' magazines, meetings, conferences and so on. These activities represent a mix of formal and informal communication. Since electronic media blur the distinction between the formal and the informal, they offer a flexible approach of particular interest to societies. In the print era, commercial publishers concentrated primarily on producing journals. They are now having to consider whether they need to diversify their functions in an electronic era, so as to compete with society services. Some are already trying to provide added-value services round the journals they publish. This diversification of provision can also be found in other types of serial, such as magazines or newspapers. Though the print version remains basic for these, the electronic version offers additional attractions. For example, it may provide hyperlinks to other relevant sites, or provide a backfile of previous issues that can be searched.

Conclusion

It is clear that print and electronic publications each have good points and bad points. Authors and readers appreciate being able to access electronic journals rapidly from their own desk. They like the power to access large quantities of information, that can be searched quickly and yet takes up little space. At the same time, lengthy on-screen reading is disliked, the equipment is less portable than a printed journal, and the software involved is not fully standardized. Moreover, factors such as the difficulty of guaranteeing the long-term lifetime of electronic journal files lead to caution in their use.

The current solution, as we have seen, is to run the print and electronic versions in parallel, so that readers can use whichever version is more appropriate for a particular purpose. Judging by the reactions of researchers when questioned, such dual publication is likely to be required for some time to come. The consequent need to operate hybrid libraries, which can handle both printed and electronic resources, will be a major burden on library and information staff. As a consolation, at least it means that such staff have a continuing rôle to play, despite increasing individual access to networked resources. The cost of serial publications, even if electronic publication reduces prices, will still demand institutional purchasing, with consequent centralized control on access. This will presumably be provided by the library or information centre. Moreover, as both information technology and electronic serials continue to change rapidly, many readers will need assistance in finding and handling information. Hence, the impact of electronic serials on library and information staff may well be to increase their workload and the scope of their task.

References

Brock, W H (1980) The development of commercial science journals in Victorian Britain. In Meadows, A J (ed) *Development of science publishing in Europe*, Elsevier Science Publishers.

Cameron, G (1998) Electronic databases and the scientific record. In Butterworth, I (ed) *The impact of electronic publishing on the academic community*, Portland Press.

Ginsparg, P (1998) Electronic research archives for physics. In Butterworth, I (ed) *The impact of electronic publishing on the academic community*, Portland Press.

Helal, A H and Weiss, J W (eds) (1996) *Electronic documents and information: from preservation to access*, Essen University Library Publication No 22.

King, D W, McDonald, D D and Roderer, N K (1981) *Scientific journals in the United States*, Hutchinson Ross.

Manten, A A (1980) Development of European scientific journal publishing before 1850. In Meadows, A J (ed) *Development of science publishing in Europe*, Elsevier Science Publishers.

Meadows, A J (1993) Too much of a good thing? Quality versus quantity. In Woodward, H and Pilling, S (eds) *The international serials industry*, Gower Publishing.

Moline, S R (1989) The influence of subject, publisher type, and quantity published on journal prices, *Journal of Academic Librarianship*, **15** (1), 12–18.

Page, G, Campbell, R and Meadows, J (1997) *Journal publishing*, Cambridge University Press.

Russon, D and Campbell, R (1996) Access to journals, *Logos*, **7** (2), 178–85.

Zuckerman, H and Merton, R K (1971) Patterns of evaluation in science: institutionalization, structure and functions of the referee system, *Minerva*, **9**, 66–100.

2

How and why serials are produced

Sally Morris

Introduction

This chapter concentrates on the mechanics, and the economics, of journal production, and is written largely from the publisher's point of view.

The chapter begins with a resumé of some characteristics of a journal, together with some observations on the needs of authors and readers. The value added by the publishing process is then analysed. Different types of journal publisher are outlined, and there is a general examination of the specific tasks and the overall management processes undertaken by publishers, followed by a brief look at the economics of journal publishing. Copyright and rights management lead on to a final section detailing some of the opportunities and threats facing the publishing industry in these uncertain times.

The journal

A journal is not simply a physical collection of articles, printed on paper and bound into an issue for ease of use. The journal collects contributions together under a recognized title, which acts as a convenient 'shorthand' for a number of messages about the content, such as its *coverage*, *quality*, and *editorial slant*. The journal signifies a particular subset of all possible articles, especially relevant to a given community.

1   A good journal title conveys an explicit message about subject *coverage* (this may be broad or extremely narrow, depending on the journal). To those familiar with the journal from past experience, it is even more meaningful.
2   The next thing the reader wants to know is whether the article is worth reading – its *quality*. Appropriate journals provide a guarantee that the article has been through the respected processes of peer review and refinement

until it is fit to publish. The 'pecking order' of journals is well understood by the communities they serve, and is objectively, if somewhat crudely, indicated by its 'impact factor', defined in the previous chapter. Familiarity with a journal will also show the level of editorial quality control – for example, improvement of unclear language, correction of non-standard spellings, redrawing of illustrations, verification of references.

3   The names of the *editors* and editorial board members will give the reader an indication of what to expect in terms of types of article, and sometimes of the general 'school of thought' of the journal. Editors are human, with their own interests and preferences.

Journals also provide 'quantity control'. No reader can keep up with all the articles published in his or her field, not even with all the relevant and good articles. A journal has to be selective: in the print world, it is usually restricted to a page budget. It is often argued that electronic journals are free of such constraints. This is not entirely true. While page limits may disappear, the finite availability of people – referees, editors – will continue to act as a limit. In any case, it is highly questionable whether unlimited quantity is really a benefit to the reader.

Authors and readers

Journals are essential for both authors and readers. The same person may operate as both, in different modes, but each has different requirements.

Many writers and speakers (eg Parekh, 1998), and a recent large-scale survey (Swan and Brown, 1999), have made it clear that authors want:

- credit for their research – promotion, tenure and research funding all depend on publication in the 'right', high-quality, heavily cited journals
- speed – rapid dissemination of their work, particularly important when there is a 'priority race', most commonly in science
- wide distribution to the appropriate readership
- quality – publication in a highly respected, peer-reviewed journal
- retrievability – their work must be readily found by those to whom it is relevant
- citability – they need their work to be cited by others; this is a crucial measure of academic success
- permanence – available, unaltered, for future researchers.

In some subjects, particularly those with substantial practical or commercial applications – such as engineering, chemistry or medicine – there are two groups of readers. There are researchers themselves, who both read and write research papers. There are also practitioners, who are heavily dependent on the research of others, but do not themselves carry out research or publish papers.

The first group, researchers, wants the following:

- relevance – the ability to home in on research in precise areas
- breadth – at the same time, researchers want the ability to scan the contents of a wide range of journals to retain an awareness of the wider context
- quality – peer review, although flawed, is still widely accepted as the best method of filtering to achieve this
- retrievability – the ability to find and obtain appropriate articles quickly and easily, whether in a known journal or via a wider database or web search
- speed – readers want to know about new research as soon as possible
- wide availability at minimum cost, preferably free at the point of use.

Non-researchers have similar needs to researchers, but with the following differences:

- They may have little time for browsing in a wide range of journals, and place more emphasis on search and retrieval.
- Cost may be less of a problem since they are usually working in a better funded, commercial environment and the link between appropriate information and increased profits is obvious.

The way that these needs are satisfied can differ quite widely between different types of communities, depending on a number of factors, including *subject*, *community size*, and *technology use*.

1   A *subject* community such as high-energy physics, which consists entirely of researchers, is much better able to communicate informally than is the community in an 'applied' subject area such as medicine. In addition, there are subjects like pharmaceuticals where the majority of research cannot be published until a patent has been taken out on the work. This has an obvious impact on speed of publication. In non-experimental subjects, one researcher's work neither builds directly on, nor proves or disproves, previous work; the body of knowledge grows in a more cumulative way. Speed of publication may be less important, but access to earlier, sometimes centuries earlier, work can be essential.

2   Another significant factor is the size of the author/reader *community*. The smaller the community, the more readily its members can communicate informally – by personal communications, by conference presentations, by

preprints. Below a certain community size, it is also likely that researchers know each other's work and reputation, and can estimate quality fairly readily.

3   Communities also differ in their use of new *technology* – not so much 'whether' as 'what' and 'how'. Different communities tend to use different types of computers and, therefore, computer software: consider the popularity of Unix in the computing field. Particular text-processing tools are suitable for specific disciplines, eg TeX for mathematics and physics. Some fields are remarkably disparate. For example, in biology, authors use a wide range of software, and the recently mooted creation of a physics-style preprints database in the biomedical sciences (PubMed Central, 1999) might be very much more difficult.

The publisher's contribution

Where a publisher really adds value for information users is not so much in the practical tasks it performs as in its far more important 'invisible' functions:

1   Selection and collection – the publisher, usually with the aid of an outside expert editor, obtains the right content, evaluates it, and gathers it together.
2   The journal 'brand' – in addition to the 'shorthand' function of a journal title, the publisher's imprint can also carry certain messages about the character and quality of its publications. However, publishers are well aware how rarely readers can identify the publisher of a journal.
3   Quality control – both the outside editor and the publisher have an important responsibility for ensuring that the material published is of good quality. In addition to the quality of the content, publishers pay attention to the quality of its expression.
4   Presentation – reading and retention of text, tables and illustrations is made substantially easier by the right layout and design.
5   Navigation – tables of contents, section headings, abstracts, indexes and page references are important both for print journals and in providing navigational links on the world wide web.
6   Retrieval – accurate and explicit article titles and abstracts are essential for retrieval when searching appropriate database services. The provision of relevant metadata and metatags for online retrieval via the web is also becoming important. More generally, the publisher must ensure that the journal is included in those databases which are most commonly consulted by the relevant researchers. This can also convey a significant quality message, as inclusion in the most prestigious services is not automatic. It can

take several years before a new journal is included in *MEDLINE* or ISI's *Current Contents*.

The nuts and bolts of publishing

Many people would be hard pressed to define what publishers do; there is widespread confusion between publishers and printers. This section outlines the different types of publisher, and the specific tasks and management processes which they undertake.

Types of publisher

There are essentially three different types of publisher:

1 Learned societies, assisting the process of scientific communication in their discipline. See Chapter 1 for their rôle in the development of the journal. They usually provide copies of their journals free or very cheaply to members. Surpluses from their journal publication programme go back into the broader activities of the society.
2 University presses, normally a department of, or owned by, the parent university. Profits go to support the activities of the university in general.
3 Commercial publishers, owned by shareholders, who ultimately benefit from the proceeds. Many societies work with either university or commercial presses in order to obtain the best professional service and financial return for their journals.

Journals management

The journals programme

The publisher will mesh its journals in with its other activities, such as book or database publishing. A publisher of both books and journals may find that there is valuable cross-fertilization – of ideas, of authors and editors – between the two. The publisher needs to keep a healthy balance between journals at different stages of maturity: not launching too many new journals all at once, however good; not being too dependent on journals which are in decline. Profitable, mature journals will help to support those which are new and not yet profitable, or those which are still valuable but declining. A publisher which handles journals on behalf of others (for example, learned society journals) has to be particularly careful not to become too vulnerable to a large proportion of its business being taken elsewhere at short notice.

The management process

Unlike books, journals are managed continuously, and improvements can be made all the time. The number of pages can be increased or decreased, design can be changed, the mix of content (perhaps to include review articles or bibliographies) can be altered, prices are reviewed every year. The journal publisher is continuously monitoring not only the data available from the editorial office and the subscription system, but also information from the marketplace about journals in general, and about the individual journal in particular. Questionnaires to both actual and potential authors and subscribers may be repeated every few years. Customers who have cancelled their subscriptions can be particularly valuable sources of information about what the publisher is doing wrong. Journal management is relatively rarely a matter of dramatic changes, more a question of continuous touches on the tiller.

When a journal goes electronic, however, very many additional possibilities present themselves:

- linking to and from secondary databases, references in other journals, supporting data
- inclusion of non-printable material such as sound, video, executable programs, animations or three-dimensional diagrams
- addition of features such as discussion lists, table of contents alerting services, facilities for bookmarking or annotation.

The possibilities are endless, and expensive. The skill lies in identifying which are actually of such value to customers that they will pay for them.

New journals

Despite the pressure on library funds, new journals continue to be launched. There are still new areas of research which are sufficiently significant to require their own journal. The creation of a journal is one of the milestones in the creation of a distinct discipline or sub-discipline. Sometimes these new areas arise through the overlapping of fields previously seen as unrelated, as biochemistry arose between biology and chemistry. Other new areas may arise through increasing specialization or 'twigging'.

Commissioning editors spend much time listening, reading and talking to their customer communities. Literature searches will help to indicate whether papers on a particular subject are growing in number, appearing in a wide variety of journals, or appearing in journals in widely separated disciplines. Once a possible new journal has been identified, the publisher carries out extensive market research to establish its value to the community it aims to serve. It is usual to survey 50 to 100 workers in the particular field to discover whether they think that the journal has been correctly conceived, who should edit it, who should be on the editorial board, whether they would contribute to it, and whether they would recommend their library to buy it even if it meant cancelling another title. Only a small proportion of new journal ideas ever come to fruition.

If the journal goes ahead, the publisher will seek out the appropriate editor or editors and editorial board members, and provide the support they need. Publishers usually pay for office equipment and secretarial help, and frequently for office space. The publisher will also provide guidelines – on how to manage peer review correctly, how to keep track of manuscripts at various stages of review and revision – and may provide software too.

The journal cannot be launched without papers. An 'Announcement and Call for Papers' will be mailed to suitable lists, including contributors to related journals and members of appropriate societies. In addition, the editor and editorial board will be extremely active in inviting people to contribute. Key authors may be commissioned to write important articles for the launch issues, in order to establish the intended profile of the journal. When the journal is close to publication, flyers will be sent to appropriate mailing lists, including subscribers to related journals; advertisements will be placed; materials will be exhibited at relevant meetings and conferences.

Marketing and sales

Marketing is vital for journals. To sell a journal, the publisher needs to spread the word in the right way to the right people. Publishers also have to deal with such matters as discounts to subscription agents and others, handling of claims, customer service, and selling both via intermediaries and directly to customers.

Publishers usually deal with subscription agents when selling their print journals to libraries. In some countries, eg in parts of Europe, the same rôle is taken by booksellers, while in others, such as Japan, the agent takes on a very much larger rôle and provides a comprehensive service to the library. Both for the library and for the publisher, the subscription agent simplifies the 'many to many' relationships, turning them into 'many to one to many'. Renewals information is now supplied to the publisher on magnetic tape in most cases, which considerably reduces the need for keying, and the risk of error, at both ends. Most publishers give the agent a discount off the published price in return for their services. If they do not, the agent normally has to add a service charge to the library. A publisher will have commercial relationships with most if not all of the major subscription agents. Publishers usually prefer to deal with their personal and membership subscriptions directly, although if the customer requests it they may go through an agent, commonly at no discount.

The journal issue

We now move on to cover the processes involved in processing the individual paper and producing a journal issue in a little more detail. See Page, Campbell and Meadows (1997) and UKSG (1994) for more information.

Submission and review

When researchers have completed a piece of work, they write it up for publication. The article is submitted to the highest quality journal in the field in which the authors feel they have a reasonable chance of publication. Authors are asked not to submit their work simultaneously to more than one journal. If the journal editor considers the article to be potentially suitable for publication, he or she will approach two or more referees. Referees are normally anonymous, but are usually credited by, for example, acknowledgment at the end of the volume. Referees will check that the research is sound, the work original, the conclusions sufficiently significant to be worth publishing, and the language adequately clear and unambiguous. The referees will recommend that the editor reject the paper, accept it unconditionally, or – in the majority of cases – request changes, as a condition of acceptance, or for resubmission of the article.

Editing

Once the paper has been accepted for publication, the editor may edit it further for language and style. The publisher will then carry out further copy-editing and proof-reading, checking use, and spelling, of language and specialist terminology once more, and that each article is laid out for ease of navigation by the reader. Reference citations may also need to be checked for accuracy. In academic and professional publishing, unlike trade publishing, editorial intervention is usually relatively minor, but consistency and accuracy of, for example, numerical information can be crucial. In addition, extra features may need to be added to electronic journals, such as internal and external links. Copy-editing is one function which can readily be carried out by freelance workers, under the supervision of the publisher.

Typesetting and preparation

When the article is ready, it is sent for typesetting, usually by a specialist company. Increasingly, authors produce their manuscripts on a word-processor, which should in principle remove the need for re-keying. Publishers often find, however, that by no means all authors' files are usable. Most commonly, articles are sent for typesetting as soon as they are ready, rather than waiting for a complete issue's worth of articles. When the article has been typeset, proofs are sent to the publisher and editor, and normally to the author as well. The copy-editor will collate all the corrections, and provide a marked-up copy for the printer to make the final corrections.

For electronic publication, the files have to be put into an appropriate format such as PDF or HTML. The electronic files must be carefully checked for accuracy, as it is surprisingly easy for errors to creep in when they are converted. Each file will need appropriate identification. Systematic procedures are absolutely essential. The files may in fact be mounted, and more sophisticated access provided, by another publisher or dedicated service provider.

Speed of publication is generally important to authors. So too is knowing what is happening. The publisher tries to keep the author informed about the progress of the paper. Online systems, which authors can consult for themselves, are one way of achieving this. One of the main reasons why speed is so important to authors is the question of priority, and published versions often include the date of acceptance and sometimes the date of submission.

Issue make-up

Once papers have been edited, typeset and corrected, the assembly of the journal issue can begin. The editor will select, from those papers available, the most interesting and balanced issue, bearing in mind that articles need to be published, as far as possible, in order of acceptance. In addition to the papers themselves, there will be other elements – a table of contents, possibly editorials, book reviews, letters to the editor, perhaps advertisements. For a print journal, this should add up to a multiple of eight or 16 pages for economical printing.

Advertising and reprints

The income from advertising, or, in the case of medical journals, for example, the bulk sale of copies of particular articles to commercial companies, can provide a useful adjunct to subscription revenue. In extreme cases it can make the subscription price very low indeed. Advertising sales is a very specialized area, often undertaken by freelances. Bulk reprint sales require both a good understanding of the content of the articles and excellent contacts with the companies concerned.

Production

Very few publishers do their own printing and binding, but close liaison with the printer ensures that everything goes to schedule, and that each issue is published on time. If using an external supplier to mount electronic journals, equally close liaison is required.

Despatch to subscribers

Printed journals are either sent to subscribers directly from the printer, using labels supplied by the publisher, or they are delivered to the publisher's or a third party's warehouse from where this is done. The choice of despatch method will be based on both speed and cost, although overseas subscribers find it very irritating to receive a topical journal long after their domestic counterparts. Although electronic journals are not physically despatched to subscribers, the decision still has to be taken to make certain files available on a certain date. There may also be an e-mail alert to advise subscribers that new content is available.

Offprints

After the journal itself has been sent off, the printer will assemble the offprints which have been requested by authors. This can be a labour-intensive and costly process, and publishers have been reducing the numbers of free offprints provided to authors, on the assumption that photocopying and preprint distribution were taking their place. Surprisingly, however, the recent Association of Learned and Professional Society Publishers (ALPSP) survey (Swan and Brown, 1999) indicates that authors still value offprints highly as a method of communicating their work.

Single and back issues

Publishers receive a small but constant flow of orders for individual journal issues, in many cases to fill a gap in a backrun. The handling cost is relatively high, so the pro-rata subscription price is usually marked up to some extent. After a while, handling older back issues may not be worthwhile for the publisher, so specialists often take on the remaining stock and pay the publisher a proportion of the proceeds from sales.

Tracking and record-keeping

Throughout the entire publishing process, publishers need to keep extremely detailed and accurate records of individual journal articles, to know what stage each article has reached, and for rapid retrieval, essential for both print and, especially, electronic publication. Details of article authors must be kept, for speedy communication, and to check that the necessary agreement forms have been completed. Subscription fulfilment systems, managing very large numbers of customers subscribing in advance, either direct or through an intermediary, at various different rates, to different combinations of titles, must be maintained. Electronic journals introduce new complications. Records are required for individual end-users – if password security is used, or if individually tailored services are provided – or for IP addresses. Additional complexity arises if print issues are supplied via an agent's consolidation service, but electronic access requires knowledge of the end customer.

The economics of journal publication

The economy of learned journals is a very peculiar one, and is a matter of great discussion and controversy at present. Traditionally, research authors have never been paid for publication. There has been a mutually acceptable 'quid pro quo' whereby publishers obtain the right to publish articles, and researchers obtain funding and career advancement through publication, together with a number of free offprints of their article. In some instances, predominantly in the USA, authors have been required to pay for publication, in the form of either submission charges or page charges, though this is becoming less common. Authors of other kinds of articles, however, such as review articles, are frequently paid a fee. While it would be perfectly possible to pay fees to journal contributors, this would of course make journals more expensive, unless taken out of existing payments to editors and societies; rising journal prices are already a cause of concern.

In addition, referees carrying out peer review have not normally been paid, though they usually receive a free subscription to what may be a very expensive journal. They have been satisfied to do this for the good of their discipline, and a certain amount of prestige. Journal editors nowadays are very rarely unpaid. At the very least, their (and their university's) expenses will be covered, and an honorarium or royalty in addition is not uncommon. When a journal is published on behalf of a learned society, the society normally shares in the profits, or alternatively receives a very substantial royalty. An informal survey of publishers suggested that, overall, the percentage of journal revenue paid out in expenses, fees, honoraria and royalties was very similar to, and sometimes more than, the percentage paid to book authors and editors.

Since neither authors nor referees are routinely paid, commentators, including academics, librarians, and university administrators, sometimes query why publishers should be paid for journal subscriptions and thus enabled to make a profit. As already outlined, publishers do, however, create the journals which authors and readers find valuable. This work does have a cost.

Another unusual thing about journal finances is the way the cash-flow operates. The customer pays up-front for the whole year, and the publisher spends the money throughout the year (although new journals require substantial expenditure before the first issue is published). Thus the publisher starts the year with a large positive balance, which is gradually reduced throughout the year until what is left at the end is the profit. This is a significant element in the financial attractiveness of journals to publishers. If it were to be modified, for example, by the wholesale adoption of individual article sales in preference to subscriptions, the financial profile would be very much less attractive. For books, it works the other way round – the publisher spends the money first, and sells the books later. Thus journals can be an important way of helping a publisher to fund its other publications.

Publishers have to set subscription prices at levels which will enable them to cover their costs and make some surplus or profit. The costs which have to be covered include:

- direct costs – eg typesetting, printing, binding
- overheads which can be allocated to the individual journal – eg editorial costs, marketing
- overheads which cannot be individually allocated – eg management, ware-housing, journal fulfilment
- development costs – eg investment for electronic provision.

As with the pricing of any product, publishers need to price high enough to make the journal viable, but not so high that sales are seriously reduced. Some of the costs (editing, typesetting, overheads) are fixed irrespective of the number of copies; others (paper, a proportion of printing costs, postage and packing) vary directly with copies. Thus even if a publisher believed that by halving the price of a journal, the subscriptions could be doubled (very unlikely!), the publisher's costs would increase and so profits would be less than before. Having once set a subscription price that makes sense for a new journal and its market – possibly including lower prices, based on the marginal production cost, for society members or individual subscribers – the subscription price is reconsidered every year. This has to be done before mid-year – long before the publisher is likely to know final details of page extents or costs – in order to provide prices to subscription agents and libraries in good time for the following year's renewal process. Several factors need to be taken into account, including cost increases and growing page numbers. Once a journal starts declining, and losing subscriptions year on year, the publisher has an additional problem in trying to balance the books. Increasing the price still further in order to compensate for the loss of subscriptions can easily lead to a 'vicious spiral' of further subscription cancellations, but failure to compensate will make the journal less and less profitable until it has to close.

Copyright and rights management

Once an article is accepted, the author will be asked to grant the publisher the rights to publish it. Most publishers ask authors to transfer copyright for reasons of administrative convenience, although an exclusive grant of licence, transferring all publishing rights, is a legally acceptable alternative. An increasing number of publishers, particularly learned societies, are not now requesting transfer of copyright, but simply a grant of publishing rights. ALPSP has issued a model 'Grant of Licence' to facilitate adoption of such policies. The author will also be asked to confirm that the work is original, has not been published elsewhere and is not in breach of anyone else's rights. The forms which publishers use, commonly known as Copyright Transfer Agreements, usually grant back to the author, or employer, various rights to use and distribute their own work (eg in classroom teaching or conference presentations), provided this does not unduly damage the publisher's sales. In addition, authors frequently want to mount articles on an intranet or a web page. Publishers are becoming more relaxed about this, provided that the usage is non-commercial and full reference is made to the original publication.

Increasingly, publishers are requesting electronic as well as print-on-paper rights, since more and more journals are being published electronically as well as in print. Even if a publisher does not yet publish an online version of a journal, it may well want to produce archival CD-ROM versions, and may be approached for permission to reproduce individual articles, or extracts of articles, in other publications which will appear in both print and electronic format. The publisher may also want to sign licences with other services to make journal contents available digitally, whether directly or for specific purposes such as document delivery or archival access eg JSTOR (Butler, 1999). If an individual author refuses to grant such rights, the publisher may refuse to publish the article, as they cannot deal in whole journals if the rights status differs from article to article.

Publishers have a moral responsibility to protect their authors' rights – to protect their work from misappropriation or distortion and to act against any infringements, whether or not the author has transferred copyright. Such infringements can be made easier by electronic delivery, and publishers have to be clear in their customer licences about what is and is not permitted, and vigilant in detecting and ending any abuse. Technical protection, such as encryption or digital watermarks, is expensive but publishers sometimes feel it is appropriate to use it.

Publishers need to deal with rights in journals as well as books. It is rare to sell foreign language rights in a whole journal or even a journal article, and when it happens the price is usually rather low: it is more a question of getting the content into a market it would not otherwise reach, such as China. More frequently, however, the publisher is dealing with requests for permission to reproduce individual articles, or parts of articles, in other publications or for educational purposes. Authors want their work to be as widely and freely available as possible. Publishers therefore try to take a generous approach to educational and research re-use by others. Permission is usually granted free of charge to the author to re-use his or her own work, and in many cases there is no charge made for educational use, or to other publishers who undertake to grant free permission to reproduce their own copyright material in return. Even when charges are made they will be fairly low. This means that it is a time-consuming, but not revenue-generating, operation. A share of what revenue there is may be passed to the society or editor as part of their royalty. It would not normally be practicable to pass it to individual authors and agreements with authors normally transfer full rights to the publisher. However, many publishers do distribute a share of the income from substantial subsidiary uses, such as bulk sales of reprints.

In the UK, copies of print journal articles can be made, under certain conditions, without infringing copyright, for 'research or private study', as laid down in the 1988 Copyright, Designs and Patents Act. Requests for copies from the British Library Document Supply Centre, and other similar sources, have to be signed by the requester to certify that copies are indeed for 'research or private study'. Guidelines on the meaning of 'fair use' in the copying of electronic, as opposed to print, material have recently been agreed between UK publishers and universities (PA/JISC, 1998). Publishers are naturally nervous that this use could be expanded to the point where journal subscriptions themselves were threatened. The UK Copyright Licensing Agency (CLA), and its counterparts in other countries, have set up schemes to license universities and other institutions to permit them to do more than this limited amount of photocopying. More substantial copying, eg for course packs, can be cleared via the CLA Rapid Clearance Service (CLARCS). New CLA licences will permit the creation of digitized copies (Copyright Licensing Agency, 1999). These licence arrangements can simplify matters for both the user and the publisher. Payments are distributed to publishers at regular intervals.

Opportunities and threats for publishers

This final section of the chapter considers some of the current issues and controversies which concern publishers.

The 'library crisis'

Publishers are very familiar with the apparently insoluble economic problem confronting journals and libraries. More research is done and the researchers want to publish their work. More journals are published, and existing journals get fatter. The total cost of the available information rises, while library budgets do not keep pace. In consequence, libraries can buy a smaller and smaller percentage of the information their users require, and are moving more and more towards access, eg document delivery and interlibrary loan, as opposed to acquisition. This leads to declining subscriptions for individual journals, which in turn fuels price rises as publishers try to keep their income steady.

The principal driver is the growth in research papers. The number of researchers increased by 100% between 1975 and 1995, and so did the number of articles published (Tenopir and King, 1997). Virtually all research eventually gets published somewhere. Some contributes to the increasing number of pages in established journals, and the rest helps to fill the new journals that are created to satisfy specialized interest groups. However, funding to acquire the results of research has not increased at the same rate as research funding itself, and the problem is particularly acute in universities. In the USA, federal funding for scientific research and development increased by over 200% between 1976 and 1996 (National Science Foundation, 1997). Over a similar period, 17 major academic libraries in the USA experienced a reduction in library expenditure from 9.8% of instruction and departmental research expenditure in 1976 to 8.8% in 1990 (Mellon Foundation, 1992). This, combined with journal price rises, leads inevitably to journal cancellations. The articles which are needed are obtained through other channels, such as commercial document delivery or interlibrary loan, which brings no revenue to publishers, though it does have a real cost to the libraries, estimated at $30 per article (Brown, 1997).

Falling journal subscriptions make it more difficult for journals to stay in business. If prices are maintained, the journal becomes less and less profitable. If prices are increased, in order to share the fixed or 'first copy' costs – typically a high percentage of total costs – over a smaller number of subscribers, the problems become more acute for customers. Journals do not appear to compete primarily on price, but on quality and relevance. The experience of some UK learned society publishers who attempted to hold prices down some years ago was that it made absolutely no difference to the rate at which subscriptions declined. This vicious spiral must be broken somehow, if the benefits which journals bring to the research community are not to be lost.

Electronic journals

The Internet and the universal adoption of the world wide web have made it possible to distribute research more widely. It was originally hoped that this would also reduce the costs of scholarly communication. The initial investment costs for publishers are, however, huge, and systems need continual development, by expensive staff. Ongoing costs do not appear to be very much lower than for traditional print publishing (Shaw and Moore, 1996; Shaw and Elliott, 1998). Furthermore, while authors and subscribers still want the security and permanence of print alongside the electronic version, costs actually increase.

Advantages of electronic journals which are often suggested include:

1 International reach – although readers all over the world can in theory read an electronic journal article, if they have the appropriate equipment, the real question is whether people will access it in the first place. To do so, they will need to know of its existence and its website address. This requires international promotion, although more direct links between databases and journal articles may also help.

2 Speed of publication – as soon as an article is ready for publication, it can be published, and is immediately available to readers. Many of the important processes of publication, however, will not in themselves be speeded up. Peer review and subsequent revision are often the most time-consuming steps between submission of an article and its eventual publication. Similarly, the editorial processes are at least as time-consuming as for print. Additional work may also be required such as adding links, supplementary material, etc.

3 Additional capabilities – electronic media make it possible to do more with research information, for instance, linking backward and forward between references and articles, using video and moving images as illustrations, etc. Colour illustrations may be prohibitively expensive in a printed journal, but present no such problem in an electronic journal. Appropriately used, these features can make research papers more useful and interesting. However, they require new skills in authors and additional expense for the publisher.

4 Reduced costs – obviously, an electronic-only journal saves all the costs associated with printing and delivering a paper copy. However, for the relatively small print-run of a typical academic journal, print and delivery costs represent a small proportion of the overall costs, while all the editorial and 'first copy' costs stay the same, and the costs of administration and data handling usually increase. Tenopir and King (1999) estimate that the overall saving for a journal with 500 subscribers is no more than 4%, though it could be as high as 25% if there are 5000 subscribers. These figures may not take full account of increased computer-related costs for larger circulation journals. If the publisher decides to offer both print and electronic versions, savings will be less, but the new, electronic, costs will remain the same. Overall, Tenopir and King estimate that costs may increase by approximately 20%. This is therefore an expensive option, although many publishers have found that their readers are as yet unwilling to go without print copies.

5 Convenience – one of the great advantages of an electronic journal is access from the user's own desktop. There is no need to go to the library, and risk finding that someone else is using the required journal issue. In the UK, this was highlighted by the SuperJournal project as being the key feature which users of electronic journals value above all others (SuperJournal Project, 1999).

6 Searchability – another key benefit of electronic journals is the ease with which the reader can search for articles, browsing the tables of contents of previous issues, for example, to find a hazily remembered article, or searching for particular words or phrases. This hugely improves retrieval compared with looking through every issue in turn on the library shelf.

7 Linking – publishers are increasingly adding live hyperlinks to the journal material, such as links to articles cited in the reference list. Links to and from databases such as *MEDLINE* are becoming commonplace, at least to the abstract of the cited article. Access to the full text depends on whether this been enabled for users at that institution. Developments of universal electronic identifiers such as the Digital Object Identifier (DOI) (Baron, 1997; Paskin, 1997, includes useful glossary) are greatly simplifying the process of linking. A number of publishers have recently announced a new initiative, Crossref, which will operate in conjunction with the International DOI Federation to link references between journal articles from the participating publishers' titles (Reference linking service announcement, 1999).

Issues raised by electronic journals

Article by article, or issue by issue

With electronic journals, articles can be published individually, when available, and some publishers are now releasing articles in their pre-publication form. Publication of an article as quickly as possible can be very helpful to the author, particularly in fast-moving science disciplines. However, it is not necessarily helpful to readers, who may still prefer to receive, whether electronically or on paper, a collection of articles packaged together in a journal issue. Article-by-article publication also raises some difficult issues. What is the official 'publication date' if the electronic version is available before the print version? How are pre-publication versions distinguished, if they are not quite the same as the published version?

Pricing

Pricing electronic journals is very difficult. For print journals, publishers can estimate subscription numbers fairly accurately, and know whether they are increasing or declining. They know how the market reacts to more or less steep price increases. They know what costs their income has to cover. With electronic journals, there are none of these certainties, and furthermore no publisher yet knows what long-term effect electronic journals will have on print subscriptions. One of the reasons many publishers begin by offering the electronic version free of charge is because they simply do not know what the uptake will be.

It seems logical to say that the subscription price is the price of the content, regardless of medium, although some publishers would argue that customers will pay a little more for the extra convenience, and additional functionality, of an electronic version. This would argue for a pricing model based on the print subscription price, possibly plus a small electronic surcharge, and very commonly with a discount if both print and electronic versions are taken together.

There are further considerations. Some publishers' larger institutional customers take multiple print subscriptions to key journals, to serve different sites, or even buildings, within the same organization. With an electronic subscription, those multiple subscriptions could disappear. It may seem fairer to vary the subscription according to the size of the user-base. Publishers are experimenting with many different possible pricing models, but their underlying objective is to stay in business – to continue to generate enough income to more than cover their direct costs and overheads.

Licensing

Selling electronic journals, whether singly or in packages, involves selling rights rather than physical objects. There are rights involved even when a print journal is bought, but these are comparatively well known and understood. So each electronic journal sale requires a licence, in effect a contract for a rights transaction. In simple cases, such as personal subscriptions, the licence may be standard and it may be possible for the customer simply to click an 'I Agree' button to accept the terms. However, when licensing a number of journals to an entire institution or consortium, the process is much more complex and involves detailed explanation and negotiation. This is creating a huge new workload for both publishers and libraries, often including the involvement of expensive lawyers on both sides.

One of the difficulties for libraries is that every publisher has a different form of licence, which, even if it allows or forbids the same things, will say so in completely different words. In the UK, the Joint Information Systems Committee (JISC) of the government-funded Higher Education Funding Councils, and the Publishers Association (PA), have worked together to produce a 'model licence' (PA/JISC, 1999a) for electronic journals in university libraries; other groups are working to create similar models for other kinds of library. Each publisher, and library, will not be able to use a completely identical licence, but the model does provide useful building blocks: standard definitions for words such as 'site' or 'authorized user'; a standard order of clauses; wording which can be lifted or adapted to suit particular needs. A further recent attempt to issue suggested model licences, with different models for use by single academic libraries, academic consortia, public libraries, and corporate and other special libraries, has been undertaken by John Cox Associates in conjunction with five of the leading subscription agencies (Welcome to Licensingmodels.com, 1999). A listing of a large number of model licensing initiatives, which is periodically updated, can be found on the ALPSP website .

Individual article supply

In the new environment, it is incontestable that readers acquire articles from electronic journals one at a time, and that no single reader will want to acquire every article in a journal. In addition, just as in the print world, customers will want to supplement their journal holdings with individual articles from other journals. However, publishers fear that if individual articles are available instantly, in perfect copies, through 'electronic interlibrary loan', this might dramatically erode subscriptions. One proposal, which has been put forward by another PA/JISC working group (PA/JISC, 1999b), is to provide at least partially automated electronic document delivery for 'ILL' purposes, at the same price as at present, but for part of the income to go to the publisher. It is hoped to test this proposition in a pilot project, to be undertaken by a research team from ingenta and the University of Lancaster.

For now, it is difficult for publishers to decide whether to sell individual articles at all, and if so how to price them – too low and subscriptions will be threatened, too high and no one will buy them. Some publishers are beginning to offer individual articles to non-subscribers, and it will be very interesting to see what effect this has. The PEAK (Pricing Electronic Access to Knowledge) trial of Elsevier Science journals at the University of Michigan is a current example of this (Mackie-Mason et al, 1999).

Intermediaries

Many publishers initially wish to deal direct with their customers for the sale and licensing of electronic journals. They want to learn at first hand what their customers' needs and wishes are. However, customers are making it very clear that they would prefer to acquire electronic journals, as they do print journals, through subscription agents or other intermediaries. The agent can often take over the task of explaining the variety of different licences which publishers offer, though not necessarily of negotiating the final terms. Actual purchasing is obviously simpler for the customer – they can pay the agent one cheque, in their local currency. The agent's system will enable users to access all their electronic journals at a single website, which is preferable, for the user and the library, to the alternative of having to visit a different site, with different access controls, for each publisher.

In addition to traditional subscription agents, there are other kinds of intermediaries in the electronic journals world:

- those who mount electronic content on behalf of others, such as Catchword or HighWire Press
- providers of centralized access control mechanisms, such as ATHENS
- aggregators that combine content and sell it as a single package, such as Ovid.

Some combine one or more of these functions.

Archiving

This issue is dealt with in more detail in Chapter 7 below. There is no easy way of archiving an electronic-only journal. Even if the archiving library makes back-up files of the journals, these may need to be updated over time, as technology changes. Links to other sites – one of the attractive features of online journals – may become inactive due to the impermanence of URLs. In addition, not all publishers may wish (or be able, within their system) to continue to make access available to backfiles even when the library has stopped subscribing. Indeed, libraries themselves have increasingly favoured the notion of 'access' rather than 'ownership', and the leasing or licensing of information for a finite period, rather than its outright purchase. At present, legal deposit of electronic materials is not required in most countries. In the UK, government intends to make this a legal requirement by about 2002: a pilot scheme is currently being developed.

New models for scholarly communication

It seems clear that the existing model for selling research information in the form of journals will have to change. Logically, if the amount of material being published and thus the overall cost of information continues to increase more steeply than the money available to purchase it, then sooner or later something has to give. Both publishers and librarians are keen to ensure that any transition to a new way of doing things is achieved without losing the real strengths of the present system, such as quality control, via peer review and editing, and journal identity. There is no guarantee, however, that either publishers or librarians as we know them will have the same rôles – or even any rôles at all – in a new system.

Some of the new models being tried involve freely accessible preprint servers (Harnad, 1995), such as that for physics and related disciplines set up by Paul Ginsparg at Los Alamos National Laboratory, in which authors can deposit their work. They are encouraged to replace the preprint with the final published version when it is available. It appears that journals which in effect provide the quality control and journal identity for these freely available papers have not, so far, suffered from lost subscriptions (Smith, 2000). There is current controversy over a proposal to set up a similar archive for the much wider field of the biomedical sciences under the auspices of the US National Institutes of Health (PubMed Central, 1999). These suggestions are sometimes combined with the proposition that authors, or their university employers, should retain copyright control of their articles, and that they should then make them freely available to the research community.

A related proposition is that authors, rather than subscribers, should pay for the costs of peer review and editing, with financial input either from research funds or from library savings (Harnad, 1998). Unlike the traditional system of page charges, it is argued that this could make journals completely free of charge to readers, which would achieve the maximum visibility for authors. A few publishers are already experimenting with this model – for example, the

Institute of Physics Publishing has launched the *New Journal of Physics* (Haynes, 1999). The most difficult issue to resolve is the migration of the existing journals environment – authors, research funding bodies, libraries, publishers – from the current situation to any new paradigm. A summary of many of these proposals or experiments in free or low-cost non-commercial alternatives to the present system is given by Rowland (1999).

Another promising way forward – less revolutionary – lies in novel approaches to selling and pricing journal information. Good examples are the UK National Electronic Site Licence Initiative (NESLI) (see Chapter 5) and Academic Press's IDEAL service, where libraries can pay for electronic access to all Academic Press journals, and then buy print copies of selected titles at a 'deep discount' price of 25% of the standard print subscription. A number of enterprising publishers are trying to rethink the whole financial model, rather than attempting to replicate that for print subscriptions which may well be unviable in the long term. Some publishers positively welcome licensing to consortia, and see it as a way of increasing access to their journal material at incremental cost. Others are beginning to grapple with new ways of scaling prices according to the number of users, or use levels, models more familiar in the database sector. Yet others separate out a basic fee for access to the database, with additional fees for print and/or electronic subscriptions. An increasing number are offering discounts to consortia, on the basis that a single licence negotiation reduces time and overhead costs, as well as increasing the market. The Association of Research Libraries in the USA, under the SPARC (Scholarly Publishing and Academic Resources Coalition) initiative, is encouraging the establishment of new, cheaper, journals, mainly through the learned societies, to compete with certain expensive commercially published titles.

Completely new financial models may well be the way forward, although experimentation will be risky and will take courage on all sides. It can be more difficult for established players to adopt completely new ways of doing things, and new entrants to the marketplace may have an advantage in this time of change. Existing publishers have shareholders, or society members, who expect a constant, and increasing, stream of financial returns. It is impossible to guarantee this if the business model changes completely, perhaps selling individual articles 'by the drink', and/or selling licences rather than physical containers, with simultaneous heavy investment to move into high-value electronic publishing.

The challenge for publishers

What do publishers, old or new, have to do to merit a place in the information chain of the future?

1   First of all, publishers have to *understand their markets* intimately: know what their customers do, how they do it, and how they use information to help them – by asking the right questions, listening, reading and learning.

2   Then publishers need, in the hackneyed phrase, to *'add value'*. In this case, that means very specifically that they have to make information well worth the price that they ask customers to pay for it. When adding new features to electronic journals, they have to be sure that customers actually believe they are worth additional cost. If something is not 'value for money' in the eyes of the customer, it is hard to argue that it has any value at all.

3   Next it is essential that publishers ensure that *customers* not only know about the existence of their journals and how to get them, but also *understand* what value has been added to the information. This is not always easy to convey, but it is vital.

4   Finally, publishers have to find ways of *selling* their publications to customers which are acceptable, and indeed helpful, to them. It is entirely possible that this will mean moving away from existing pricing models, such as journal subscriptions, and trying out radically new and untested models in their place.

If they do all this and more, publishers old as well as new will have an important part to play in the electronic future. If they do not, evolution will no doubt take its course.

Note

This chapter draws heavily on a number of previous publications by the author:

Morris, S (1998) Learned journals and the communication of research, *Learned Publishing*, **11** (4), 253–6.
Morris, S (1999) Who needs publishers?, *Journal of Information Science*, **25** (1), 85–8.
Morris, S (1999) Getting started in electronic publishing. Introduction to *Reader on electronic journal publishing*, INASP.

References

Association of Learned and Professional Society Publishers (ALPSP)
    http://www.alpsp.org.uk
ATHENS
    http://www.athens.ac.uk/
Baron, J (1997) Why we need information identifiers, *Learned Publishing*, **10** (2), 132–4.

Brown, D (1997) Exorcising the spectre of inter-library loans, *Learned Publishing*, **10** (3), 207–19.

Butler, D (1999) Preserving paper for posterity, *Nature*, **397** (21 January), 198–9.

Catchword
   http://www.catchword.co.uk/

Copyright, Designs and Patents Act 1988, HMSO.

Copyright Licensing Agency
   http://www.cla.co.uk/

Copyright Licensing Agency (1999) *CLA and the digitization of text*, available at:
   http://www/cla/co.uk/www/digital.htm

Digital Object Identifier system (DOI)
   http://www.doi.org/

Harnad, S (1995) Universal FTP archives for esoteric science and scholarship: a subversive proposal. In Okerson, A and O'Donnell, J (eds) *Scholarly journals at the crossroads: a subversive proposal for electronic publishing*, Association of Research Libraries, available at:
   http://www.library.yale.edu/~okerson/subversive.html or
   http://cogsci.soton.ac.uk/~harnad/subvert.html

Harnad, S (1998) Learned inquiry and the Net – the role of peer review, peer commentary and copyright, *Learned Publishing*, **11** (4), 283–92.

Haynes, J (1999) New Journal of Physics: a web based and author-funded journal, *Learned Publishing*, **12** (4), 265–70.

Highwire Press
   http://www.highwire.org/

IDEAL (Academic Press)
   http://www.idealibrary.com/

JSTOR
   http://www.jstor.ac.uk/

Los Alamos Eprint Archive
   http://xxx.lanl.gov/

Mackie-Mason, J K et al (1999) A report on the PEAK experiment: usage and economic behavior, *D-Lib Magazine*, **5** (7–8), available at:
   http://www.dlib.org/dlib/july99/mackie-mason/07mackie-mason.html

Mellon Foundation (1992) *University libraries and scholarly communication.*

National Science Foundation (1997) *National patterns of R&D resources.*

NESLI (National Electronic Site Licence Initiative)
   http://www.nesli.ac.uk/

Ovid
   http://www.ovid.com/

Page, G, Campbell, R and Meadows, J (1997) *Journal publishing*, Cambridge University Press.

Parekh, A (1998) The view of a scientist-author. In *Economics, real costs and benefits of electronic publishing in science: proceedings of the ICSU Press workshop, 31 March to 2 April 1998*, available at:
http://associnst.ox.ac.uk/~icsuinfo/confproc.htm

Paskin, N (1997) Information identifiers, *Learned Publishing*, **10** (2), 135–56, available at:
http://www.elsevier.nl/homepage/about/infoident/

Publishers Association and Joint Information Systems Committee (1998) *Guidelines for fair dealing in an electronic environment*, available at:
http://www.ukoln.ac.uk/services/elib/papers/pa/fair/

Publishers Association and Joint Information Systems Committee (1999a) *Model licence between UK universities and publishers*, available at:
http://www.ukoln.ac.uk/services/elib/papers/pa/, or
http://www.library.yale.edu/~llicense/Pajisc21.html

Publishers Association and Joint Information Systems Committee (1999b) *Request for proposals: pilot project for the supply of electronic documents, complementing 'inter-library loan'*, available at:
http://www.jisc.ac.uk/pub99/jp-edd-mainrfp.html

PubMed Central
http://www.pubmedcentral.nih.gov.

PubMed Central: An NIH-operated site for electronic distribution of life sciences research reports (1999), available at:
http://www.nih.gov/welcome/director/pubmedcentral/pubmedcentral.htm

Reference linking service announcement (1999), available at:
http://www.library.yale.edu/~llicense/ListArchives/9912/msg00004.html

Rowland, F (1999) Electronic publishing: non-commercial alternatives, *Learned Publishing*, **12** (3), 209–16.

Shaw, D and Elliott, R (eds) (1998) *Economics, real costs and benefits of electronic publishing in science: proceedings of the ICSU Press workshop, 31 March to 2 April 1998*, available at:
http://associnst.ox.ac.uk/~icsuinfo/confproc.htm

Shaw, D and Moore, H (eds) (1996) *Electronic publishing in science: proceedings of the joint ICSU Press/UNESCO expert conference, February 1996*, ICSU Press/UNESCO.

Smith, A P (2000) The journal as an overlay on preprint databases, *Learned Publishing*, **13** (1), 43–8.

SPARC (Scholarly Publishing and Academic Resources Collection)
http://www.arl.org/sparc/

SuperJournal Project (1999) *Summary of SuperJournal findings: readers*, available at:
http://www.superjournal.ac.uk/sj/findread.htm

Swan, A and Brown, S (1999) *What authors want: the ALPSP research study on the motivations and concerns of contributors to learned journals*, ALPSP (summarized in *Learned Publishing*, **12** (3), 170–2).

Tenopir, C and King, D W (1997) Trends in scientific scholarly journal publishing in the United States, *Journal of Scholarly Publishing*, **28** (3), 135–70.

Tenopir, C and King, D W (1999) *The transformation of scholarly journals: 20-year trends in the economics, use and information-seeking patterns of scientific print and electronic scholarly journals*, Special Libraries Association.

UK Serials Group (1994) *Serial publications: guidelines for good practice in publishing printed journals and other serial publications.*

Welcome to Licensing models.com: model standard licences for use by publishers, librarians and subscription agents for electronic reasons (1999), John Cox Associates, available at:

http://www.licensingmodels.com

3

Serial information delivery options

Hazel Woodward and Mick Archer

Introduction

Once upon a time (actually not that long ago) the life of a serials librarian was reasonably straightforward. Although print-based serials encompass a wide range of different types of publications – journals, newsletters, newspapers, technical and research reports, yearbooks, annuals and national and international government publications – and despite the fact that they have a wide variety of publication frequencies, the printed, or indeed microfilm or microfiche, serial is a known quantity. There are set procedures for selecting and acquiring titles – much of the work in this area has traditionally been handled by a subscription agent. Manual or computerized systems are in place to receive and check in individual issues and the physical item can be displayed on a shelf – easily accessible to the end-user. After an agreed period of time current issues are collected together and stored or bound to form a permanent archive for future generations of scholars. Occasionally, when pressures on space become acute, decisions need to be taken on replacing printed back runs with microform collections. How simple that life sounds now!

So what has caused this situation to change? The answer is, of course, the rapid and pervasive developments in IT which have facilitated the publication and delivery of serials information in electronic format. Mainstream journal publishers (commercial publishers and learned societies alike) can, and do, publish parallel print and electronic versions of their titles. Print-based versions can be dealt with by libraries in the time-honoured manner but their electronic counterparts are causing a great deal of consternation among serial librarians. There are a number of frequently asked questions:

- Can they be purchased separately from the print version?

- Can they be ordered via a subscription agent, or via library purchasing consortia?
- Should they be catalogued on the library OPAC?
- How do libraries alert their users to the fact that a serial title is available electronically?

These and many other questions are currently being addressed by serials librarians worldwide.

Free material

But commercially produced electronic journals (e-journals) – usually with a print-based equivalent – are only one part of the changing serials environment. There are also many thousands of e-journals and e-newsletters freely available on the Internet. Usually published by enthusiastic individuals or small groups, these titles are intended for distribution to a specific, focused consumer group and can be of recreational, vocational or academic nature. Unlike commercial journals whose revenue stream depends on library subscriptions, these titles have no subscription costs and do not require libraries to be part of the information chain. Nevertheless, they do contain useful and relevant information for many areas of academic study and are therefore of interest to librarians. Many of the UK subject gateways such as EEVL (Edinburgh Engineering Virtual Library) and SOSIG (Social Science Information Gateway), now coalescing into a combined Resource Discovery Network (RDN), include links to those freely available Internet journals and newsletters. Once again a plethora of questions remain unanswered:

- How do libraries find out about titles?
- Is it necessary to provide access via a library interface?
- How can they be controlled given that their birth and death rate is very high and they have a propensity to move sites fairly frequently?

Aggregation

It is clear from the questions raised above that e-journals have introduced a new level of complexity to serials management. However, e-journals as separate, discrete publications are only a part of the new scenario. Once in electronic format, the published 'issue' of a journal can very easily be split up into individual articles. Of course, this also holds true with paper-based journals, and inter-library loan photocopy services have traditionally fulfilled the need for individual article delivery. However, in the electronic environment the whole process can be significantly speeded up and articles can be delivered to the scholar's desktop at the press of a button – provided that the appropriate payment is made either by the individual or the institution. There are a growing number of aggregators in the information world who are offering web-based full-text databases containing searchable bibliographic information backed-up by full-text e-journal articles. Many of these databases are subject-oriented, for example, Gale's *Business ASAP International* for business and management information and the Institute for Scientific Information's (ISI) *Science Citation Index*, which is available via a number of different aggregators and interfaces. A small number of aggregators use CD-ROMs as a publishing medium for full text, for example *ADONIS* – owned and originally developed by Elsevier, but including approximately 900 medical, pharmaceutical and chemical journals from a number of publishers – and Bell and Howell's *Business Periodicals Global* – containing the full text of over 400 journal titles (available in CD-ROM and web versions).

Copyright

The situation is further complicated by electronic copyright issues. Copyright dictates that each aggregator must negotiate with each individual journal publisher to obtain permission to mount the electronic text of articles on a network. As some publishers will not grant permission, or their material is prohibitively expensive, most full-text databases do not contain the full text of *all* articles indexed by the service. There are many implications for libraries which subscribe to such services:

- Which journals are available in full text?
- What back issues are available?
- How are additions and deletions notified to the customer?
- What is the payment model – an annual subscription to the database, or is access contingent upon a subscription to the print or electronic journal?
- Should the titles in the database be added to the library OPAC?
- Where the service and OPAC are web-based, should links be established?

Planning delivery strategies

The various strategies for delivering serial information to the end-user must be addressed by a library's strategic plan, and operational issues (*how* it is done) should be encompassed in a collection development policy. Serials are an extremely important and expensive resource and, as several surveys demonstrate, they are consistently ranked as one of the most important information sources for researchers and academics (Tenopir and King, 1997). Most academic, commercial and industrial libraries continue to spend a high proportion of their materials budget on printed serials, up to 80% in some academic libraries (LISU, 1998). Currently, e-journals and other serial-based electronic resources only account for a small proportion of most material budgets – in UK universities, for example, this proportion is about 10%. Figures for special (or workplace) libraries are much more difficult to determine as statistics are not collected in any organized way. However, given the general remit of such libraries it can be reasonably assumed that increased speed of delivery of electronic information – particularly full text – to the desktop is a high priority for leading edge research and development companies. For all libraries, the pace of change is likely to accelerate as teaching and learning methods change in schools and further and higher education institutions, and as the implications of government strategy on lifelong learning begin to impact on all types of libraries and information services. Business, research and academic cultures are also facing rapid change as the IT revolution advances.

For libraries 'the skill of the collection manager will be to create collections which balance the best features of print and electronic resources, and which make them work together effectively in the interests of the library user' (Breaks, 1999). In exercising these skills the library manager must make informed decisions about the rate of change that is acceptable within their organization. Should library policy attempt to speed up the transition from print to electronic information particularly if there is articulated resistance from users? Such issues must be addressed by the strategic planning process. Much useful information – transferable to a wide range of different library environments – can be obtained from the hybrid library projects currently funded by Phase 3 of the UK's Electronic Libraries (eLib) Programme (eg HyLife Project, HeadLine Project), in turn funded by the Higher Education Funding Councils' Joint Information Systems Committee (JISC).

In an ideal world, libraries would operate within organizations that have established an information strategy. UK academia does at least have the JISC guidelines for developing such a strategy (JISC, 1995). The developing Distributed National Electronic Resource (DNER) (Russell and Dempsey, 1998) aims to establish a managed national collection of electronic information sources which can:

- support academic research
- support undergraduate and postgraduate teaching and learning
- provide better support for the management of information systems.

However, no such guidelines exist for commercial, industrial or public libraries. Therefore, as few organizations have information strategies, it is up to the library to devise a collection development policy and strategy that will guide it towards the provision of a focused group of resources to support the mission of the organization. It is only when such a policy is in place that librarians can have a clearer sense of *what* information should be provided and *how* it should be delivered and accessed.

What information should be delivered?

The ultimate aim of the library is to deliver *relevant* information to the end-user as *quickly* and *cost-effectively* as possible. For centuries the traditional model has been for libraries to provide core printed journals on the shelves in the library building. However, if a paper copy of a title is delivered to the library, is this really delivering information to the user? When is the information delivered? When it is available on the library shelf or when it is with the user?

Information about information

Many libraries had, and some still have, 'circulation list' procedures to facilitate information use. However, there are differing opinions about the effectiveness of circulation for the delivery of serials information. If a journal issue is being circulated to users, is it being used or is it simply unavailable to other potential users? To get around this problem some libraries stopped circulating journals and offered to supply photocopies of tables of contents to users who requested them. More recently, many libraries have withdrawn their paper-based service and provide users with electronic table of contents services such as *UnCover* or *SwetsScan*. Ironically, although useful tools for alerting users to potential articles of interest, contents page information rarely provides sufficient information about the *content* of an article.

Librarians acknowledge that delivering bibliographical information supplemented by abstracts of articles is a far more useful service to users than basic contents page information. In the past, the service was known as Selective Dissemination of Information (SDI) and was an important element of the library service in commercial and industrial libraries. Printed bulletins were distributed to scientists and researchers providing them with up-to-date information about articles received by the library. The reason that it was not adopted on a large scale in other types of library was that, as a manual process, it was extremely labour-intensive. All this has changed, however, with the advent of the PC and networked electronic databases.

It is not an exaggeration to say that electronic databases have completely revolutionized end-user current awareness and retrospective searching activities. Stage one of the revolution was the migration of print-based abstracting and indexing (A & I) services to the electronic environment. Online searching of electronic databases – despite the fact that it was complex and expensive – enabled librarians to provide more effective and faster SDI services to users. Stage two of the revolution was the delivery of the same data – but with a new 'user-friendly' search interface on CD-ROM. Early CD-ROM implementation involved the provision of databases from designated PCs within the library. For the first time, end-users were able to perform their own information searches – even if they did have to visit the library to do so. More recently hardware and software have developed to network CD-ROM databases but this has created an enormous amount of additional work for library systems staff. Much CD-ROM software was initially designed for standalone applications and networking features have been added as an afterthought. Consequently, each CD-ROM supplier has developed their own unique networking software which often requires a great deal of manipulation to adapt to local computer setups. In addition:

- Expensive hardware has to be purchased to run the CD-ROM network.
- In libraries with a large collection of CD-ROMs, work associated with updating the system with new discs is considerable.
- Some suppliers add a substantial networking charge to the base subscription price depending on the number of concurrent users.

The advantage of CD-ROMs is that they have a known annual subscription cost and once purchased – along with appropriate hardware – can be searched many times without incurring additional costs. However, because of the high staff and hardware costs associated with CD-ROMs, the migration of many electronic information sources to the web is a welcome development. It must be remembered, however, that for libraries to deliver web-based information services, a pervasive and reliable organizational IT infrastructure is a necessity.

Libraries are now able to deliver a variety of services to the user's desktop. All the major A & I services, such as *INSPEC, Biological Abstracts (BIOSIS), Index Medicus (MEDLINE), Psychological Abstracts (PsycLit)*, are available, although there is still a more comprehensive range for the sciences than for the humanities. Moreover, as the range of aggregator services expand, so do the services that come with them. Many aggregators, for example ingenta and OCLC, offer current alerting services whereby end-users set up their own information profiles based on either specific journals or keywords. Bibliographical information (often with abstracts) about articles which match this profile is then delivered to the user's e-mail box. So far, so good, but as all librarians are aware, knowing what information is available is only the first stage; what users *really* want is the information itself.

Full text

Significant factors in the delivery of full text are the facilities and equipment available to the end-user. If a serial is subscribed to in paper format in the library then users of that library can access the information in it – always assuming that the library is conveniently located for their place of work and open long hours, the required issue is not lost, vandalized or at the binders and they can read the language of the content! Lorcan Dempsey recently commented (in a paper presented to the 1999 UK Serials Group Conference) that libraries are very good at 'hiding printed serials information on the shelves' (Dempsey, 1999; see also Dempsey, Russell and Murray, 1999). For many years we have confused our users by providing only minimum information about journal titles held by the library in our catalogues and providing indexes and databases of journal articles, with no indication of which are held by the library. However, it is encouraging that the management of, and access approaches to, the growing mass of currently unconnected electronic resources provided by libraries is under discussion at the highest levels of the information profession. The 6th MODELS workshop addressed just these issues (Russell and Dempsey, 1998). The MODELS Information Architecture (MIA) is a framework for discussing distributed information resources with a shared vocabulary and set of concepts. MIA assumes an environment in which users access resources through 'gateways' of 'brokers', for example, the ROADS (Resource Organization And Discovery in Subject-based services) cross-searching software, which brokers access to the various subject gateways. What is common about these systems is that they present the user with a 'landscape' which hides some of the underlying differences between resources; they also collate results and support a higher quality of service than unmediated access.

A further factor in the delivery of full text is the availability of delivery systems. If journals are only made available electronically, then only the people who have the technology can access them. An important issue for librarians to consider is whether electronic delivery might inadvertently disenfranchise a significant section of their user population. Even when technology is made available, the variation in access and quality and equipment will differ between types of institution. A large pharmaceutical company will probably have up-to-date computer equipment readily available to all staff, whereas an academic institution may have PCs on all staff desks but students and researchers may only have access from shared computer laboratories. This variation between technology-rich and technology-poor users will affect not only access to electronic information but also how information sources are used. If most information is supplied through an intranet and users have fast computers with printers attached, then printing articles may be more prevalent. However, if users only have access to remote printers shared by large numbers of students and frequently out of paper or jammed, then reading on screen may be a preferred option.

A decision about the delivery of full text will also be influenced by the time criticality of the information. In many fast moving areas of research, it is vital to know the results of other similar work as quickly as possible. Significant costs can be incurred in duplicating work already done; conversely, significant savings can be made by getting it right first time. In this case, speed of delivery of information is vital. In other areas speed might not be so vital but comprehensive coverage or cost-effective assured delivery might be important factors. Even when only paper journals are considered, such factors can affect delivery decisions. Should foreign journals be delivered by airmail? Would the use of a consolidation service in the country of origin of the journals be more effective and reliable? If speed is not vital, would consolidated supply of all titles – with the more effective claiming procedures this allows – better ensure comprehensive acquisition?

Subject coverage

Clearly the subject coverage of serial information must reflect the requirements of end-users. A research-led university will attempt to provide a range of scholarly journals, subject-focused bibliographies and full-text databases to support all its major research areas, whereas a small college library – which has teaching as its primary mission – is likely to provide a range of more general serials supplemented by broader-based full-text databases accessible either on CD-ROM or via the web. (Technological infrastructure will clearly affect these choices.) A commercial or industrial library, on the other hand, will need to support specific areas of research which may change at relatively short notice and such a library is unlikely to have the responsibility of maintaining archival holdings of titles in specific subject areas. Special libraries may also be required to deal with commercially sensitive or classified information, for example, libraries in the aerospace or defence sectors, or those based in legal practices or firms of management consultants. Providing access to, and secure delivery of, such information is a serious issue for librarians.

What is certain is that no library can hope to acquire (either in print or electronic format) all the serials information required by its clients. The best that can be done is to acquire and provide quick and easy access to core information and set in place procedures for users to obtain access to their wider information requirements – either from document delivery services or by utilizing reciprocal access agreements with other information providers.

Quality information

Quality control is a key issue for librarians. A pharmaceutical company library or information service, for example, must provide quality information to its research scientists as rapidly as possible to enable the scientists to develop new products, stay ahead of competitors and, above all, make a profit for shareholders. In these times of anarchy on the Internet, librarians must play a key rôle in maintaining the quality of information. There is some concern in academic institutions that many school and undergraduate students are 'surfing the net' for information for their course work with scant regard for its source, accuracy or quality. Derek Law notes the spectre of the student Internet users 'who think they have the whole answer when they do not' (Law, 1997). It must be remembered that it is the *content* that is the important element, not the delivery medium. It is all too easy, in these exciting times of electronic delivery, to subscribe to e-journals because we are aiming at a 'critical mass' of journals to get clients using them, when, if we had critically reviewed the content, we would not have subscribed to the printed version.

Usage

Another factor that requires careful consideration is user preference as regards reading information on screen or on the printed page. The received wisdom is that most people prefer reading anything longer than one page in paper format. Various studies demonstrate that users who locate an article in an e-journal that they wish to read, print it out (Woodward et al, 1997; SuperJournal Project, 1999). The usage of serials literature can also vary according to subject area and this should be taken into account when deciding what information should be made available in what format. An article published in the humanities, with theories developed throughout the text, might be read sequentially in order to understand the flow of the arguments. The abstract would contain a summary of the final conclusions, thus helping the user decide whether to read the full text. In the scientific area, sequential reading is less common. Scientific literature is often read in a more selective way: the abstract may be read first, then the conclusions, then the diagrams or tabulated data. On the whole, sequential reading is easier using the printed page whilst, given suitable navigational aids, non-sequential reading can just as easily be carried out on a computer screen. Whilst these are very rough generalities they are further factors which need to be taken fully into account when selecting the method of delivery of serials information.

Delivery options
The traditional journal model

Having considered the issues above, what are the options for the delivery of serial information? Let us deal with a straightforward case first. If a library has responsibility for the archival holding of a journal, or of journals in a specific subject area, most librarians would agree that a subscription to a paper copy is essential. The reason for this is the uncertainty of electronic archiving at the present moment. Most publishers will not take responsibility for the archival holding of their e-journals on their servers, claiming that archiving has never been their traditional rôle. Some will offer cumulative CD-ROMs of their titles but this is not a satisfactory long-term solution for libraries for a number of reasons. First (as discussed earlier in the chapter) the cost of CD-ROM networks in terms of staff time, hardware and software is high. Secondly, library users do not have the time or the inclination to learn to use a multiplicity of different interfaces in order to access individual journals. (The only way this might work would be the use of a service such as *ADONIS* as an archiving system, so that only one interface needs to be learned and supported.) The third reason is the transient nature of computer technology. CD-ROM technology is already old and, particularly when the music industry moves on to a new technology, the equipment to read and archive will become more difficult to obtain. Much, however, depends on the cost of local storage and cooperation on standards among publishers. If CD-ROMs were to be used solely as a transport medium and the documents were then stored locally on ever more economical hard discs – with the added advantage that locally held documents could be made available in a standard format – this could prove a cost-effective archiving solution.

Meanwhile, archiving is recognized (by JISC and other national and international bodies) as being a major, unresolved issue in the development of electronic full-text services. It is to be hoped that initiatives such as the eLib CEDARS Project (CURL Exemplars in Digital Archives) will provide guidance for libraries in best practice for digital preservation.

Assuming that the archiving issues *are* resolved, there is little doubt that many libraries will deliver an increasing proportion of full-text serials information in electronic format. The major advantages of electronic delivery are well known – 24-hour desktop access, speed of availability, and ability to search both the metadata and the full text. The process of delivery is, however, less clear-cut. Should the traditional model of delivering a known journal with its comfortable, familiar features of contents pages, issue and volume numbers be maintained in the electronic environment? This is certainly how most publishers perceive the future and, indeed, it is the model adopted by purchasing consortia such as OhioLINK in the USA and the National Electronic Site Licence Initiative (NESLI) in the UK (Woodward, 1999). Libraries continue to purchase a known product for their users – often still tied to the print subscription – and publishers transfer the economic model of subscriptions into the digital library, along with their handsome profit margins. Although most purchasing consortia are negotiating discounts for their members, such discounts rarely (if ever) overcome the 'serials crisis' facing most libraries. Demand for serials inevitably exceeds the ability to pay for them. The main problem for libraries, currently, is that users are still demanding that print subscriptions be maintained; thus money cannot be freed from the materials budget to build the critical mass of e-journals necessary for the successful marketing and promotion of the e-journals service. From a library perspective it is imperative that publishers recognize that their pricing structures must become more flexible. Print subscriptions must be 'unbundled' from electronic subscriptions and digital articles must be made individually available either on a pay-per-view basis or on a time-finite contract basis.

Individual document delivery

Print and electronic individual document delivery is, and will continue to be, an essential element of libraries' serials delivery strategy. Traditional document delivery supply services such as that available from the British Library Document Supply Centre (BLDSC) still have an important rôle to play. With urgent action faxed documents delivered within two hours and even standard delivery direct to users available in two to three days, this is a very efficient and cost-effective way to supply journal information. The major abstracting and indexing services are now also developing services to make full text accessible through their databases. In the past this service has been supplied by setting up, or linking to, traditional paper-based document supply systems. Nowadays, electronic supply is being developed with either the journal text being stored on the intermediary's server or links established to the publisher's site. Examples include the *ABI Inform* full-text service *ABI (ProQuest)* and *Applied Science and Technology Plus*, which provides a full-text service for *Applied Science and Technology Index*.

Although most libraries regard the journal literature as essentially the province of the researcher, there is a growing demand for electronic texts for teaching and learning purposes. Traditionally libraries have catered for the demands of large numbers of students requiring access to the same journal arti-

cles by obtaining copies of such high demand articles on interlibrary loan –
copyright cleared – and placing them in a 'reserve' or 'short loan' collection.
Phase 2 of the eLib Programme had a number of projects examining the question of 'electronic reserve/short loan collections' – among them Project
ACORN (Kingston and Gadd, 1998). This project, based at Loughborough
University, sought to provide full-text electronic journal articles linked to web-
based reading lists for the Departments of Geography, Human Sciences and
Information Science. The major obstacles to provision proved to be the time
and effort required to obtain electronic copyright permissions from publishers
(each individual publisher had to be approached directly by project staff) and
the cost and time taken to produce a high quality digital copy of the articles
(fewer than 1% of publishers approached were able to provide a digital copy of
their articles). Much was learned from the eLib Phase 2 projects and a new project – HERON (Higher Education Resources On demand) – is now continuing the work in this area. Based on a consortium of three UK universities
(Napier, Stirling and South Bank), Blackwell's Bookshops and Blackwell's
Information Services, Project HERON aims to establish a national database
and resource bank of electronic texts to widen access to course materials
(Jacques, 1999).

Alternative models

Some of the new models discussed in this section have already been mentioned
in Chapter 2, but it is still worth referring to them again in the following
paragraphs.

At the present moment it is clearly the case that print-based journal subscriptions are still the preferred delivery medium for the vast majority of academics and publishers. One might expect commercial publishers to adopt this
position, but it is regrettable that many learned societies also take this view.
Presumably, the fact that their publishing activities subsidize many of their
other membership activities is an important factor. Many academics also have
a close association with established journals – as editors, members of editorial
boards, or simply as authors – and this may influence their opinions on alternative methods of scholarly communication.

However, detractors of the current journal publishing system are prominent
and voluble and include Steven Harnad (1998) from Southampton University,
Andrew Odlyzko (1997) from Bell Laboratories and Jean-Claude Guedon
(1995) from l'Université de Montréal. Their view is that the Internet provides a
mechanism for academics to regain control over their own communication system from commercial publishers. Scholarly or 'esoteric' publishing (Harnad's
term) should become non-commercial with scholarly articles available from the

web free of charge to users. This view is, unsurprisingly, supported by many academic librarians, who regard the present system as grossly unfair. Why should, they argue, the output of academics be provided free of charge to publishers, who then charge high prices to libraries to access that material?

The idea that all scholars should 'self-archive' their own papers on their own websites, freely available to anyone in the world, is an attractive one. Harnad's concept is that any paper – regardless of whether it is unsubmitted, submitted but not yet refereed, refereed and accepted but not yet published, or published – should be mounted on the web with a statement on its current status. However, it must be recognized that, particularly in academia, many other complex factors impinge upon the model. Academic status is tightly bound up with the prestige of the journals where one is published. The prestige of a journal is dependent on a multiplicity of factors including the publisher, the editor, the composition of the editorial board, the refereeing process, and citation analysis. Furthermore, the academic status of both individuals and academic departments has a considerable impact upon funding – for example, in the UK, where funding levels are determined in part by the Research Assessment Exercise (see Chapter 4). For all these reasons, attempts to change the system are slow to take off and indeed, meet with considerable resistance from various of the above stakeholders.

A similar economic model lies behind the emergence of preprint servers. This model permits papers to be submitted to the preprint archive in electronic format, and made freely available on the server, in advance of refereeing. They are subsequently submitted to, and in the majority of cases published in, conventional journals. The largest and best-known electronic preprint server is based at the Los Alamos National Laboratory in New Mexico, USA, and was created initially by Paul Ginsparg to serve the high energy physics community. It has now expanded into other areas of physics and computer science. Other preprint servers in other disciplines are also starting up – including one in psychology (CogPrints) – actively supported by Steven Harnad. Electronic preprint archives have great value, not only to authors in obtaining speedy publication – but also to users, in enabling them to obtain articles free of charge and delivered to their desktop. They must also be having an impact upon journal sales in certain subject areas; it remains to be seen how publishers will respond. A recent development is the Open Archives Initiative (1999), which met first at Santa Fe, New Mexico, in October 1999, and 'has been set up to create a forum to discuss and solve matters of interoperability between author self-archiving solutions, as a way to promote their global acceptance' and provide seamless access to the different preprint, and other, archives now operating.

In another attempt to shake up the world of scholarly communication, the US National Institutes of Health are launching a new service, *PubMed Central*, originally known as *e-Biomed*, in 2000, to provide yet another potential archive, for articles in the medical and other sciences. Publishers are being invited to deposit articles from their journals in this archive, but it is too early to say what impact this new service will have (*PubMed Central*, 1999).

The library community itself is also advancing a variety of strategies in response to the 'serials crisis'. The Scholarly Publishing and Academic Resources Coalition (SPARC), formed by the Association of Research Libraries (ARL) in the USA, is one such initiative (Webster, 1999). SPARC is an alliance of libraries that fosters expanded competition in scholarly communication by creating partnerships with publishers who are developing high quality, economical alternatives to existing high price publications. By partnering with publishers, SPARC aims to:

- create a more competitive marketplace
- ensure that publishers who are responsive to customer needs are rewarded
- ensure fair use of electronic resources
- help apply technology to improve the process of scholarly communication
- reduce the costs of production and distribution.

The University of Kansas Provost, David E Shulenburger, advances another response. He proposes to create the National Electronic Articles Repository (NEAR), a centralized, public-domain server that would manage the intellectual property rights associated with academic publications. Whereas at present, virtually all scholarly journals require the author to hand over all rights to copyright when a manuscript is accepted for publication, in Shulenburger's proposal, the author would retain the right to have the manuscript included in the NEAR database 90 days after it appears in the journals (Webster, 1999). A further example of an initiative from USA academia is Scholar's Forum from the California Institute of Technology, involving retention of copyright by researchers and participation by universities and professional societies (Buck, Flagan and Coles, 1999). In Europe, Dutch university libraries in the UKB consortium have initiated serious discussions with publishers, issuing a press release stating that they will no longer accept 'irresponsible' price increases. With the close involvement of university academics, they are examining different models for the publication of scientific research, and inviting libraries from other countries to work with them (UKB, 1999).

Epilogue

So, in summary, what is the rôle of the librarian in serials supply and delivery? Clearly the first task is to know and understand the needs of the customer as well as the various options discussed above for the supply of serial information; then match the two to give a high quality service. There is a need to negotiate and organize access to a mix of paper, electronic and database products. These must be coordinated so that access is as transparent as possible to the end-users. OPAC software able to accommodate links to e-journals, and the cataloguing skills of the librarian, are essential to ensure that users can readily locate all titles held or available, from one single interface. If access is not integrated, users will tend to look in one place, forgetting the others and assume they have found all that is available. It must be recognized that providing integrated access might well take a significant amount of work. If an agreement is negotiated with a publisher to access all their journal titles, hundreds of new records might have to be entered. Agreements in these cases should include the supply of a set of standard cataloguing records for importation into the library system.

The management of acquisition of journals in both print and electronic format and of current awareness services is far more time-consuming than the management of access to printed subscriptions. There is also a vital additional rôle that becomes more important in the electronic environment – training. Training must be given in how to use databases, full-text services and the Internet and its tools so that effective access can be achieved by customers. It must not be assumed that just because the Internet is ubiquitous, users know how to use it effectively.

Finally, we must recognize that Z39.50 standards – which enable users to search large numbers of library OPACs in one single search – open up quick and easy access to an even wider range of information sources. The question is where to stop. It is the job of the librarian to ensure that the end-user has effective access and so we must filter, coordinate and organize the sources. This is the traditional expertise of library professionals and should not be dismissed lightly if users are not to waste many hours of fruitless search. Librarians should use *their* skills to best advantage and allow their customers to use *their* skills to perform the tasks in which they are experts – research, learning, teaching and the development of scholarship.

References

Breaks, M (1999) Management of electronic information. In Jenkins, C and Morley, M (eds) *Collection management in academic libraries*, 2nd edn, Gower.

Buck, A M, Flagan, R C and Coles, B (1999) *Scholar's Forum: a new model for scholarly communication*, California Institute of Technology, available at:
http://library.caltech.edu/publications/ScholarsForum/

CEDARS Project: CURL Exemplars in Digital Archives
http://www.leeds.ac.uk/cedars/

CogPrints (Cognitive Sciences Eprint Archive)
http://cogprints.soton.ac.uk/

Dempsey, L (1999) *Bibliographic data, metadata: it's all the same, isn't it? Paper presented at UK Serials Group 22nd annual conference/4th European Serials Conference, Manchester, April 1999.* Unpublished.

Dempsey, L, Russell, R and Murray, R (1999) A Utopian place of criticism? Brokering access to network information, *Journal of Documentation*, **55** (1), 33–70.

EEVL (Edinburgh Electronic Virtual Library)
http://www.eevl.ac.uk/

Ginsparg, P (1998) Electronic research archives for physics. In Butterworth, I (ed) *The impact of electronic publishing on the academic community: an international workshop organized by the Academia Europaea and the Wenner-Gren Foundation*, Portland Press, available at:
http://tiepac.portlandpress.co.uk/books/online/tiepac/session1/ch7.htm

Guedon, J-C (1995) Research libraries and electronic scholarly journals: challenges or opportunities? *The Serials Librarian*, **26** (3/4), 1–20.

Harnad, S (1998) Learned enquiry and the Net: the role of peer review, peer commentary and copyright, *Learned Publishing*, **11** (4), 283–92.

HeadLine Project: Hybrid Electronic Access and Delivery in the Library Networked Environment
http://www.headline.ac.uk/

HyLife Project: the Hybrid Library of the Future
http://www.unn.ac.uk/~xcu2/hylife/

Jacques, M (1999) HERON: an update on the development of the project, *Serials*, **12** (1), 55–7.

Joint Information Systems Committee (1995) *Guidelines for developing an information strategy*, HEFCE, available at:
http://www.jisc.ac.uk/pub/infstrat/

Kingston, P and Gadd, G (1998) Short loan collections, *British Library Research and Innovation Report*, **92**, 5–55.

Law, D (1997) Parlour games: the real nature of the Internet, *Serials*, **10** (2), 195–201.

Library and Information Statistics Unit (1998) *LISU annual library statistics, 1998*, Loughborough University.

Los Alamos Eprint Archive
http://xxx.lanl.gov/

Odlyzko, A (1997) The economics of electronic journals, *First Monday*, 2 (8), available at:
http://www.firstmonday.dk/issues/issue2_8/odlyzko

Open Archives Initiative (1999) *First meeting of the Open Archives Initiative*, available at:
http://vole.lanl.gov/ups/ups1-press.htm

Pubmed Central
http://www.pubmedcentral.nih.gov/

PubMed Central: An NIH-operated site for electronic distribution of life sciences research reports (1999), available at:
http://www.nih.gov/welcome/director/pubmedcentral/pubmedcentral.htm

Resource Discovery Network (RDN)
http://www.rdn.ac.uk/

ROADS (Resource Organization And Discovery in Subject-based Services)
http://www.ukoln.ac.uk/metadata/roads/

Russell, R and Dempsey, L (1998) A Distributed National Electronic Resource? MODELS workshop 6 report, 5–6 February 1998, Bath, *The Electronic Library*, 16 (4), 231–7.

SOSIG (Social Science Information Gateway)
http://www.sosig.ac.uk/

SuperJournal Project (1999) *Summary of SuperJournal findings: readers*, available at:
http://www.superjournal.ac.uk/sj/findread.htm

Tenopir, C and King, D W (1997) Trends in scientific scholarly journal publishing in the United States, *Journal of Scholarly Publishing*, 28 (3), 135–70.

UKB (1999) *Policy statement by academic libraries on the pricing of scholarly journals*, available at:
http://www.uba.uva.nl/en/projects/journals-pricing-ukb/policy.html

Webster, D (1999) *Emerging responses to the science journal crisis*. Paper presented to the 65th IFLA Council and General Conference, Science and Technology Libraries Professional Group, Bangkok, August 20–28, 1999, available at:
http://www.ifla.org/IV/ifla65/papers/062-122e.htm

Woodward, H et al (1997) Electronic journals: myths and realities, *Library Management*, 18 (3), 155–62.

Woodward, H (1999) NESLI – the National Electronic Site Licence Initiative . . . creating a bit of a disturbance, *Serials*, 12 (1), 17–20.

4

Budgeting, ordering and paying for serials

Jill Taylor-Roe

Introduction

In many libraries, the serials budget accounts for the single largest area of expenditure apart from staffing. This budget is subject to innumerable external pressures: spiralling price rises, fluctuating exchange rates and the inexorable growth of journal literature, both in print and now in electronic format. Demand for new titles is generally insatiable, matched only by users' outcry at the thought of having to cancel existing subscriptions to fund their new requirements. Library managers, fighting to maintain budgets in an increasingly competitive environment, require ever more sophisticated analyses of past, present and future serials expenditure to convince their paymasters that they are getting best value for money from this major investment. With luck, this may help them to secure a modest annual budgetary increase, although the reality is more likely to be steady state or a 5–10% cut. Small wonder then that serials invariably deserve, and receive, such special attention from librarians.

What is a serial in purchasing terms?

Before any serious attempt can be made to allocate and manage a serials budget, it is essential to define precisely what this budget encompasses. For example, in addition to traditional serials or periodicals, you might include standing orders or continuations, newspapers, technical report series, official publications series and society memberships. The serials budget may also take in the purchase of backruns, binding costs, and could increasingly extend to funding document delivery, table of contents (TOC) services and electronic journal subscriptions. The latter can trigger a whole range of additional costs, which will be considered in more depth later in the chapter. The key point is that there is no simple and universally applicable definition of what should be included in the serials budget. Practice will vary from sector to sector, and from institution to institution. What the serials manager has to do is ensure they are fully aware of, and have some degree of control over, everything that is likely to be charged under the serials account.

Balance between books and journals

Most libraries still subdivide the basic materials budget under the broad head-ings of books and journals. In the academic sector, budgets have typically been divided 60:40 in favour of serials (SCONUL, 1993), although more recent data suggests a very slight swing in favour of books, to make the ratio about 57:43 (SCONUL, 1999). However, it is important to recognize that there are enor-mous variations in this pattern, ranging from an 80:20 ratio in a heavily research-led institution, to virtually the obverse in one that focuses primarily on teaching. There are also major differences between subject areas. For example, subjects such as physics or chemistry rely heavily on serials, whereas English literature generally relies more heavily on books. Similar variations can be found in the corporate library sector. Library expenditure to support the legal profession and pharmaceutical industries is usually heavily biased towards seri-als, whereas this is much less evident in libraries supporting management ser-vices and commercial businesses (LISU, 1998). Similar variations apply in the public library sector, although in comparison with the academic and corporate library communities, serials expenditure accounts for a much less significant proportion of their materials budget. Such diversity is entirely appropriate. The serials budget must always reflect institutional objectives and take account of the specific information needs and preferences of its primary user community.

Budgeting

Budget allocation requires a steady hand and a strong heart. In endeavouring to satisfy the often conflicting demands on their finite resources, librarians must frequently combine the political acumen of Machiavelli with the judgment of Solomon. The gift of foresight would also prove useful. Why is this such a chal-lenging task?

Academic institutions in the UK still receive the bulk of their funding from central government, via the block grant from the appropriate Higher Education Funding Council. However, the Funding Councils are now allocating money far more selectively to reflect the performance of individual departments or other units of assessment in quality assurance exercises. There have also been significant changes in university management in recent years, with fiscal responsibility increasingly devolved from the centre to Deans and Heads of

Department. Although in many cases what has been devolved is responsibility for staffing, operating costs, and equipment, hard-pressed Heads of Department are increasingly querying why they should not also have control of 'their share' of the library and computing service budgets, which still tend to be allocated and managed centrally, although this is no longer universal.

Devolution has some attractions for the library, which may hope no longer to attract 100% of the opprobrium resulting from periodical cancellations. The blame may now be shared more widely with faculties and departments. More positively, closer involvement of academics in the budgeting process may make them more aware of the high subscriptions and inflation rates applicable to most serials, and more sympathetic to the thought that, for some titles, it may be more cost-effective to cancel subscriptions and rely on document delivery, thus releasing funds for badly needed new journal titles, or even for books. They should also become more aware of the limited budgets available to the library – and perhaps be in a position to argue more cogently for increased funds – and the need to balance materials expenditure on journals, standing orders, monographs and document delivery.

On the other hand, devolved budgets can lead to imbalanced collections, a lack of interdisciplinary coverage, insufficient database and reference material, and potentially very great difficulties with the purchase of bundled electronic journal packages. It is essential that the library retain a large central fund, to cope with such problems.

Formulae

Competition for funds places greater pressure than ever on the library budget holder to demonstrate that central funding leads to better overall provision of library materials, and better value for money. Traditionally, it has been more common to find an allocation formula used solely for the bookfund, but increasingly, all or part of the serials fund may be formula driven. Formulae can have many functions – they can be developed because of a desire to be more equitable, to maximize benefits over costs, and to improve library efficiency (Hutchins, 1997, 119–20). On a more cynical level, they can sometimes be used for political expediency or as a smokescreen to deflect further enquiry. Budget allocation can be at several different levels, for example faculty, department or other cost centre, but whatever unit is used, the overall strategy must reflect institutional preferences and structures.

Formulae can be as simple or as complex as you want them to be. However, they will typically take account of variables such as staff and student full-time equivalent (FTE) numbers (possibly allocating different weightings), average price of materials, and demand, with a percentage of the budget retained as a discretionary or contingency element. The latter is usually employed to allow some flexibility to respond to new or developing interests or to cover more general purchases of interest to more than one group of users. It may sometimes be necessary to include an allowance for historical precedent, particularly if you are trying to break away from an allocation pattern hitherto largely driven by cost, which typically favours expensive subject areas like science, technology and medicine over the humanities and social sciences. More recently, departments' performances in the five-yearly Research Assessment Exercise (RAE) have also begun to feature in some formulae.

Other special factors that can be included in a formula are professorial journal funds (some new appointments carry allowances for new journals), or additional funds that have been allocated from a research grant. It is essential when recording these in your formula that you note when the funding expires (money which comes in this way is usually one-off). It is also important that journals purchased with these special funds should be readily identifiable, particularly at the start of the final year for which funding is available, so that there is time to find alternative funding, or to cancel the titles at the end of the subscription year.

Table 4.1   *Resource allocation by cost centre*

Cost centre	FTE allocation	RAE allocation	Cost allocation	Demand allocation	Special factors	Total
Chemistry	17433.36	18324.54	35479.26	16810.26	6500.00	94547.42
Physics	12226.92	11656.61	26109.45	9810.24	3000.00	62803.22
Maths and statistics	14016.57	13156.59	19369.82	10010.37	3000.00	59553.35
Computing	15113.26	15320.77	17369.51	12810.79	—	60614.33
Geomatics	9309.45	15320.77	12739.63	8905.13	—	46274.98
Total	68099.56	73779.28	111067.67	58346.79	12500.00	323793.30

Table 4.1 represents an extract from a very simple allocation formula, where the unit of allocation is defined as a cost centre, and the key drivers of the resource allocation are the number of staff and student FTEs in the cost centre, the RAE rating, the cost of material purchased, and the demand made on these materials. Cost allocations have to make allowances for expensive science/technology/medicine (STM) material, so arts and social sciences departments will inevitably attract lower sums under this heading. However, this may be offset by the resources they attract under other aspects of the formula, such as RAE performance, FTEs and demand.

The basic structure of the formula has been set up using a series of linked spreadsheets, or workbooks in Microsoft Excel. Although the initial set-up may take some time, once the structure is there, it is comparatively easy to update each successive year. Spreadsheets make it easy to model different budgetary scenarios, for example, calculating the impact of different rates of inflation, or varying percentages of cuts or increases in resources. When the key variables have been updated, all you really need to do is insert the current budget and the new allocations will appear – as if by magic!

Where very expensive titles are concerned there may be an element of the allocation formula that assesses whether demand can best be satisfied by providing document delivery, either through Boston Spa or other agencies. For this to work effectively, there needs to be a mechanism which triggers a review when demand for document delivery equates to say 50% of the cost of the subscription, since if demand is sustained it may then be more cost-effective to have a local subscription. Formulae can be helpful aids to resource allocation, as well as useful political tools. They should, however, 'be interpreted with sensitivity and discretion. They are useful guides but tyrannous masters' (Martin, 1980).

Electronic journals

Currently, it is the funding of electronic journals which is posing one of the greatest challenges for library budget managers. A typical medium to large-sized academic library could now be handling between 500 and 1000 electronic journal subscriptions, many of them relating to existing print subscriptions. This is still a comparatively young market – for example, Hobohm (1997, 3) suggested that in 1997 5–10% of the total production of academic journals would either be electronic or in the process of going electronic. Consequently publishers are still experimenting with various price models, for example, electronic access bundled in free with an existing print subscription, electronic access as a surcharge, or in some cases electronic only. Both of the latter models will of course attract VAT (Value Added Tax) at 17.5% in the UK on the electronic access. Duff (1999) has identified numerous other pricing models. Electronic journal pricing is the subject of intense debate, with several authors (for example, Odlyzko, 1997; Hitchcock, Carr and Hall, 1997; Harnad, 1995) arguing that electronic journals pricing models should not be bound by those set up for print, nor should they cost as much. Whilst the print plus electronic access model still prevails in this emerging market, it is hard to see publishers breaking away from print-based pricing models. However, as more electronic only journals are marketed, this ought to lead to new and more flexible pricing models, although I doubt they will be any less expensive.

From a budgeting point of view, the challenge is not simply how to find the resources to fund electronic subscriptions. There may well be additional charges for a network licence, PC software to access the journals, and in some cases, there may be a need to upgrade PC and printing facilities, not just in the library, but in the wider user community. It would be both unfair and impractical to charge all of these extra costs to the serials budget, but they have to be charged somewhere. The decision to acquire an electronic journal subscription can therefore have much greater financial consequences than the decision to take out a print only subscription. Many libraries will now have an electronic resources budget, which given the general funding picture is unlikely to have been funded additionally, but has probably been created by transferring funds from other budget heads, such as books. Technology is changing very rapidly, but as Cox (1998, 73) and others have suggested, for the foreseeable future, we are locked into a multiple medium environment. This means that from a budgeting point of view, the divisions between traditional expenditure headings will become more blurred, particularly those dealing with resources and IT equipment.

Hidden costs of print subscriptions

Whilst electronic journals clearly have many significant new costs associated with them, we should not forget that there have always been additional costs to take account of when assessing print subscriptions. There is the cost of the staff time required to receipt and process individual issues, to handle claims for missing parts, to shelve and relegate, and invariably binding costs to be added in too. With full case binding running at around £20 per volume, you could be adding on another £60 to £100 per title for binding some of the more prolific journals. Whilst binding and shelving costs would be obvious savings if you migrated to electronic only subscriptions, it is by no means clear how the receipt and claims of electronic issues will be handled. Thus it would be naïve to assume that there would be no staff costs involved in this process, although they may not equate directly to the costs of processing print only subscriptions.

Although budgeting for serials in other library sectors may not be subject to the same constraints as the academic sector, some core concerns remain the same. Whether funding comes from the public or private sector, there are still considerable pressures on librarians to justify what they have spent and it is seldom easy to secure the money they feel they need to ensure that the interests of all their major client groups are adequately represented. Thus they must continually struggle to deploy their limited resources as best they can in the face of increasing costs and the phenomenal growth in journal literature.

Continued growth of journal literature

In 1973, *Ulrich's International Periodicals Directory* listed around 50,000 periodicals in print. The current edition lists 157,173 serials, 7000 of which have been
added since last year. It further notes that there are now at least 10,332 serials
available exclusively online or in addition to hard copy, with another 3451 serials available on CD-ROM (*Ulrich's*, 1999). There will of course be some serials
that have ceased publication over this period, but nevertheless the prevailing
trend is one of steady and sustained growth. What has fuelled this boom in
publications?

Undoubtedly one of the key factors, if not *the* key factor, influencing the phenomenal growth of journal publications is the scholarly desire to communicate.
This is not simply an altruistic wish to share the fruits of your intellectual
labours with other scholars around the globe, which can be achieved by other
methods such as conferences, e-mail etc, but is inextricably linked to the fact
that job security and promotion often depend on your publication record.
Whilst in some disciplines, notably the arts and social sciences, the preferred
form of publication may be the book, most academic publication still takes the
form of journal articles. In the UK, this 'publish or perish' scenario is exemplified by the Research Assessment Exercise (RAE), mentioned earlier in this
chapter, which explicitly relates research output (measured by the numbers of
research-active staff publishing in high quality, peer reviewed journals) to
future research income. The assessments, which have been undertaken in 1992
and 1996, with the next RAE due in 2001, have resulted in significant financial
gains for some universities, and significant losses for others. These changes are
inevitably reflected in library budgets. A further complication inevitably arises
when departments that have performed well in RAE expect their performance
to be rewarded with the acquisition of more journals in their field, whilst those
that have performed badly argue that they need more journals in order to help
them improve their ratings next time. This juxtaposition of needs often requires
the librarian to perform the budgetary equivalent of the miracle of the five
loaves and two fishes.

With more and more papers being submitted for publication, journal publishers have responded in various ways. They have increased the size, frequency
and cost of their existing publications. Sometimes, there is very little warning
of these changes. For example, in June 1999 the publishers of the journal
Cellular and Molecular Life Sciences announced that because they had so many
high quality articles which they wished to publish, they planned to produce an
additional volume between October and December at a cost of circa £400. This
was an extra cost on top of the original annual subscription. Unforeseen additional costs are always unwelcome to the serials manager, particularly when

they come late in the subscription year. And even if the extra volumes are billed as optional, they can prove hard to resist as gaps in the volume sequence will inevitably generate queries from users, and require additional editing of local catalogue records.

Another favoured ploy is to split up an established journal into more specialized parts, which can be purchased separately, although there may be a small discount if you subscribe to the whole package. This practice, commonly referred to as 'twigging', can significantly increase your serials costs, but as the parent title is already established in your portfolio, it may be hard to resist user pressure to subscribe to the split titles. If the parent title is an acknowledged brand leader, for example, *Nature*, it can be very difficult to resist requests to subscribe to related titles such as *Nature Biotechnology, Nature Genetics, Nature Medicine, Nature Structural Biology*. Another variant on this approach is 'piggybacking' or 'Trojan horses', whereby a new title is supplied free with an existing subscription for a year or so. Librarians find it hard to resist putting the free title out on the shelves for consultation, where it invariably generates interest. Thus when the free title suddenly acquires a price, it has already established a foothold in the collection and may be hard to withdraw.

Although serials librarians can and do complain about the additional volumes and unwanted extra titles, it could be argued that publishers are simply taking advantage of academia's increased output rate. But the harsh reality is that even the most well-funded library has long lost the ability to purchase every journal title that it felt it ought to subscribe to. Indeed the soaring costs of serial publications have made the review exercise, often a euphemism for the serial cutting exercise, a regular feature of library life.

Library expenditure on serials

The latest statistics produced by the Standing Conference of National and University Libraries (SCONUL) reveal that in 1997/98, UK academic libraries spent £53.9m on serials and £40.9m on books – and £11.8m on electronic resources (SCONUL, 1999). These figures encompass considerable variations, with a minimum expenditure on serials of £51,249, and a maximum of £1,692,686. What is interesting is that the minimum spending on books is now £44,754, only a few thousand less than on serials (and the maximum spent on books is now £1,725,554, more than the maximum serials spend), whereas in previous years, the difference between the two would have been rather more marked. Compare these figures with those for 1991/92, which show £22.4m worth of expenditure on serials and £15.2m on books. In the space of six years, the total expenditure on serials has increased by 141% and that on books by 169%. There are various explanations for these differences. Prior to 1993/94 expenditure on the 'new universities' (formerly polytechnics) was recorded separately by the Council of Polytechnic Librarians (COPOL). The 'new' universities typically spent a much smaller proportion of their materials budgets on serials than the 'old' universities. Now that the SCONUL statistics represent the combined academic sector, this has inevitably altered the proportional spending patterns. Inconsistencies also arise from the different ways in which individual libraries treat material such as standing orders, monographs in series, and official publications – all of which may be treated as books or serials. Whilst some of these interpretations will reflect library policy decisions, they are just as likely to reflect ad hoc historical decisions. Detailed data on corporate libraries' expenditure is harder to obtain, but the 1998 Statistical Tables maintained by the Library and Information Statistics Unit (LISU) at Loughborough University indicate an even stronger reliance on serials than in academia, with 65% of total library materials expenditure being devoted to serials (LISU, 1998). Whilst it is important to bear in mind that at best, these statistics simply show trends in library acquisitions, and that data can be manipulated to make a variety of different cases (Woodward, 1990, 43), one key point stands out. Libraries are continuing to devote significant sums of money to journal purchases, and each year, rising prices means they are buying fewer journals for their money.

Journal price rises

Serials price rises have been a major concern of libraries for such a long time there is danger that the subject now seems almost passé. Yet the concerns are as valid and as significant as ever, perhaps even more so now that electronic journals are vying for an increasing share of our budgets. Most of the major subscription agents produce annual periodical price indices, and although they make depressing reading, they are nonetheless extremely useful tools for librarians. Probably the best known of these indices for the UK is that produced by Blackwell's Information Services, from which the figures shown in Table 4.2 are derived (see overleaf).

The full set of tables gives a range of comparative data: for example price rises are shown separately for broad categories such as humanities and social sciences, and within that, by individual subject area, such as politics or economics. Tables are also given by country of origin. What these figures show is that over the last nine years journal prices have increased by a staggering 154.4%, and have consistently outstripped the corresponding Retail Price Index (RPI). This trend is borne out by data gathered by the North American Association of Research Libraries (ARL) over the period 1986–98. Their figures show that during this period, the unit cost of serials purchased by ARL members increased by 175%, while serial expenditure increased by 152%. The short-fall meant that by 1998, even with such a significant rise in serials expenditure, they were able to purchase 7% fewer journals than they could in 1986 (ARL, 1999), suggesting that more expensive titles were cancelled proportionately more than cheaper journals.

Table 4.2 *Average periodical price rises*

Year	% increase on previous year	Index	Average price
1990	12.52	100.0	£154.08
1991	8.52	108.5	£167.21
1992	14.83	124.6	£192.01
1993	7.47	133.9	£206.35
1994	22.52 *	164.1	£252.81
1995	9.93	180.4	£277.91
1996	12.08	202.1	£311.47
1997	9.26	220.9	£340.30
1998	5.25	232.5	£358.16
1999	9.45	254.4	£392.01

*There was a larger than average price rise in 1994 as a result of sterling's poor performance against the dollar and major European currencies. The fall was actually caused by sterling's crash in September 1992, but because Blackwell's had bought their currency ahead, customers were cushioned from the full impact for a year.

Creating your own statistics

It is of course important to remember that these indices are only guides to general trends, and whilst it may be helpful to quote from them when making a bid for next year's serials budget, libraries must always try to extract meaningful price data from their own serials administration system.

Table 4.3 *Journal expenditure by cost centre*

Cost centre 21: Civil engineering					
	97/98	% increase	96/97	% increase	95/96
Print journals	£55027.48	14.8	£47920.84	12.0	£42781.52
E-journals	£12620.19	44.9	£8712.58	77.0	£4922.74
Average cost	£344.67	9.5	£314.77	9.4	£287.64

Summary tables showing expenditure by cost centre are extremely useful, particularly when you can produce two or three years' worth of figures to compare. Table 4.3 shows an example. This data has several uses. It can show you which cost centres are absorbing the greatest share of the budget, highlight the most expensive subject areas, and also flag up those with the greatest expenditure on electronic journals. It can be used to support a case for more resources, or to demonstrate that a particular cost centre has been receiving more than its fair share and needs to be cut back. These analyses are extremely useful when preparing for Quality Assurance Agency (QAA) visits by UK Higher Education Funding Councils.

Table 4.4   *Journal expenditure by publisher 1998/99*

	Total cost of subscriptions	No of titles purchased	Average cost of titles	% increase on last year
Publisher A	£371550	362	£1026.38	18.5
Publisher B	£15548	25	£621.92	16.2
Publisher C	£58290	388	£150.23	9.7

Analyses of expenditure by publisher are invaluable when reviewing end of year expenditure as part of preparing a bid for next year's budget. An example is given in Table 4.4. They show which publishers are consuming the lion's share of the journals budget and highlight those whose prices have increased above the average rate of inflation. This may help the library to target titles for cancellation. With more publishers offering deals for electronic access to all or part of their portfolio (often linked to the library's current spending on printed journals), you need to be able to extract this data from your library system easily and quickly.

In the past, the financial analyses produced by library systems were rather limited. However, the current generation of systems are geared up to permit much more sophisticated data manipulation – an essential requirement for day-to-day serials management.

Factors that influence price increases

It has been suggested that scholarly publishing poses a rather challenging case for economists: it is a mature market, in which key consumers (librarians) cannot afford to acquire as many journals as they would like to. This could quite reasonably be seen as demonstrating an excess of supply over demand, which in almost any other market would lead to a reduction in supply, and/or cheaper costs to the consumer. Yet what we see is more journals being published, more subscriptions being cancelled, and prices continuing to rise. Naylor (1995,

94–5) shrewdly points out one of the primary reasons for this anomaly, noting that in most cases, demand for journals comes from the end-users, who do not have to pay for the subscriptions themselves. So because demand for new journals is divorced from possession of the economic power to pay for it, the normal self-readjusting tension between supply and demand fails to operate in this market. Thus the serials market may be uniquely predisposed to tolerate price rises, but there are other factors that play their part in the cycle.

Local experience of price increases will be governed to a large extent by the subject mix of titles. For example, libraries with a strong scientific, technical or medical portfolio are likely to find more significant price rises than those which are primarily acquiring humanities and social sciences titles. Other factors which influence price rises are the mix of publishers, country of origin of titles, and currency variations.

For many years, publishers have operated a system of differential pricing for their products. Thus the price you pay can vary considerably depending upon whether you subscribe as an individual or as an institution. The institutional rate is always the most expensive. The standard explanation for this dual or two-tiered pricing structure has been that because a library subscription is intended for multiple readership, it potentially reduces the sale of individual subscriptions, and thus needs to be pitched at a higher level in partial compensation for lost revenue. Whilst there is a certain logic to this argument, one could argue that there is no conclusive evidence that those who regularly consult the library copy of a journal would ever become individual subscribers if the library did not subscribe. Thus the justification for the higher pricing structure may be rather more theoretical than practical.

Currency exchange rates

The impact of exchange rates on library materials budgets is a complex issue, and could easily merit a chapter on its own. For those interested in the wider context and background, Fishwick's article (1986, 70–87) still provides a useful exposition. What serials librarians are particularly concerned about is the relative strength or weakness of sterling against the US dollar, and now also with the state of the sterling–euro exchange rate. Rates are important as many UK academic libraries can spend one-third of their serials budget on US journals, and another third on journals published in other European Union countries.

Publishers take account of current and anticipated currency movements when setting their prices for the coming year and will obviously aim to build in a measure of protection for themselves against major currency swings. An extreme example of this was the practice sometimes disparagingly referred to by American librarians as 'price gouging', whereby some British publishers quoted a separate, fixed, dollar price for the North American market in addition to the usual domestic and overseas prices. Whilst the publishers argued that this pricing strategy was merely designed to afford them a reasonable measure of protection against currency losses and other charges they might incur, North American librarians were understandably less than convinced by this explanation (Houbeck, 1986, 183–97). This practice was a recurrent theme in serials literature throughout the 1980s, but as Astle and Hamaker (1986, 165–81) noted, there was evidence that some of the major publishers had responded to librarians' complaints and amended their pricing for North America.

There are other ways of getting round this problem, particularly if you source your serial subscriptions via an agent. All of the major subscription agents offer consolidation services, whereby journal issues are sent directly from the publisher to the agent, who checks them in, boxes them up and despatches them to the library. The publisher does not need to be aware of the final destination of the journals, so titles can be secured at domestic rates. A variant on this process is 'box and ship' which removes the check-in and claiming elements of the service, and can therefore speed up the supply to the library.

Arguably the most complicated aspect of exchange rate fluctuations, as far as serials management is concerned, is that unless you are purchasing directly from the publisher, it is harder to predict when and how any changes in currency rates will affect your purchases. Most libraries with significant numbers of serials subscriptions choose to order them via an agent, rather than deal with several hundred individual publishers. Given that agents are routinely paying large sums of money to publishers on behalf of the libraries they service, any fluctuations in major currencies will clearly have a major effect on them. In an attempt to mitigate these risks some agents will buy ahead important currencies, notably the US dollar, when exchange rates are favourable. If they judge the market correctly, they can save themselves and their library customers considerable sums of money. Blackwell's practice of buying ahead clearly paid off when sterling dropped from a high of 1.76 against the dollar in mid-1992, to a low of 1.50 in 1993. Libraries expecting to face significantly higher price rises in 1993 were pleasantly surprised when Blackwell's price index showed this not to be the case, but of course the impact fully hit home the following year (see Table 4.2 above). Although Blackwell warned their customers that the impact of sterling's decline would not be fully manifest until the following year, there is always a danger that customers forget about this. When the impact is deferred for a year, it is tempting to think that the problem has been averted.

In reality, all of the players in the serials chain are subject to the impact of capricious changes in the world economy. Whilst all parties adopt strategies to guard against losses, all we can really do is respond to the currency changes as they arise, rather than exerting any real control over them. The problems are often exacerbated by the way in which we pay for serials. In academic institutions financial years generally run from 1 August to 31 July, with budget bids required in spring or early summer. In the public and commercial sectors this is more likely to be 1 April to 31 March, or the calendar year. There has been a long running battle to persuade publishers to give notification of price rises for the forthcoming year's subscriptions in time for subscription renewals in the autumn, and subscription agents have had some measure of success in securing firm prices for the coming year by the end of the previous September. In reality, the unusual nature of the serials subscription business, where we are paying ahead for a product which will be delivered in stages over the next 12 to 15 months, means that it is impossible to eliminate risk and uncertainty from the financial process.

Channels of communication and information exchange, such as the electronic *Newsletter on Serials Pricing Issues* and the *LIBLICENSE* website and discussion list, are now very important methods allowing serials librarians to keep abreast of pricing and other information emanating from publishers, while also enabling feedback to publishers from the library community.

Early payments

The practice of paying so far ahead for goods which we anticipate will be received over the coming year may sometimes be queried by finance officers or auditors. Although the library, in some institutions, may view early payment discounts offered by agents as a means of helping to ameliorate the impact of journal price rises, this view may not be accepted elsewhere. The finance office may disapprove of, or even forbid, this practice on the grounds that it makes more sense for the parent institution to hang on to the funds (and the interest) until payment is due. They may also have legitimate concerns about what would happen to this money if the agent went bankrupt before the publishers had been paid. In resolving these conflicting viewpoints, the library must inevitably work within the prevailing fiscal policies of its parent institution. Forward payments should not be used with any supplier who has not been subjected to rigorous financial health checks, and there should be a clear, written understanding that any funds forward paid remain the property of the library until such time as they are required for payment to the publishers.

Publishing mergers

Another factor that influences journal prices is the impact of sales and mergers in the publishing industry (McCabe, 1999). As we enter the 21st century, academic publishing is becoming increasingly focused in the hands of a few major players, such as Elsevier, Wiley, Kluwer, Springer, Taylor & Francis. Some would argue that these moves are being driven by the heavy investment in technology which publishers are having to make in order to deliver electronic journals services. Smaller publishers may find it difficult to raise the necessary capital to fund such investment. From the libraries' point of view this means that an increasing proportion of their journals portfolio is concentrated on the output of a small number of publishers. This is particularly noticeable in the sciences (Nisonger, 1998, 38). For example, Loughner (1999, 3) has noted that whereas in 1990, 54% of the University of Georgia's budget for science journals was concentrated with the top ten academic publishers, by 1999 their market share of the budget had increased to 74%. Take-overs can lead to journal title changes, cessations and mergers, which are more than likely to result in journal price rises.

Ordering and paying for serials

There are various options for acquiring serials. Libraries can order their titles directly from the publisher, and indeed some actively encourage this approach, particularly learned society publishers. Alternatively, they can source their journals by country of origin, using specialist dealers at home and abroad, or else they can centralize their subscription business though one of the large international subscription agencies. Standing orders can be included with the overall serials supply or these too can be directed to specialist agencies. The rôle of the subscription agent will be considered in more detail in the next chapter. From the purchasing viewpoint, the key priorities are to ensure that suppliers are chosen fairly but competitively on the basis of reasonable cost, high quality service and reliability. A supplier's performance should be regularly monitored and, wherever possible, benchmarked against other agencies.

When ordered direct from the publisher, subscriptions are normally subject to annual renewal. Renewal forms need to be processed promptly in order to ensure continuity of supply, and if the library has a large number of subscriptions ordered directly, this can make for a considerable amount of extra work. Alternatively, when titles are ordered through an agent, they can be supplied on a 'supply until cancelled' basis where the agent will ensure automatic renewal with the publishers, unless explicitly instructed to cancel by the library. Certainly as far as invoicing is concerned there are benefits in ordering via an agent, as there is more chance of having the invoice customized to local requirements, for example by adding library subscription numbers or cost centre codes. Also with better IT links between systems, it is now possible to transfer invoice data from the agent's system directly into the library system. However, there is a considerable amount of preparatory work to be done, as you need to ensure that every subscription entry includes the local library reference number as well as the agent's subscription number if the records are to mesh correctly.

Where orders are placed directly with publishers, there is little choice over the timing of invoices and renewal dates, and the serials librarian needs to invest a considerable amount of time ensuring that everything is up to date. Life can be much easier when ordering serials through an agent as most of the larger ones offer one-line invoices, which are usually issued in July or August for the following year. As this is too soon for all prices to be known, agents usually base their estimates on the previous year's expenditure plus an allowance for inflation. A range of discounts is offered for early payment, which can help to moderate the impact of publishers' price rises. Later in the autumn, a definite invoice will be run, giving firm prices for individual subscriptions, so that the library's records can be updated. Finally, a supplementary or 'mopping up' invoice will be produced in the early summer of the following year. This approach minimizes individual invoice handling, and concentrates activity around two key periods in the year.

Management information

Given that serials represent such a major ongoing investment for libraries and one which is subject to so many different variables, it is essential to have full and accurate management information to hand at all times. In smaller libraries, this may still take the form of the traditional Kardex file, but increasingly serials management will be automated either with a standalone system, or as part of a larger library management system. Inevitably, you have to work within the limitations of individual systems, but as a general rule, it is better to record as much information on each title as possible from the outset. Retrospective data collection is extremely time-consuming, particularly as it is likely that the missing information will have to be gathered quickly, under pressure to meet an urgent deadline.

As a minimum, serials management systems should record the following data, in addition to the standard bibliographic description:

- Source of item – eg via agent, direct from publisher, via exchange.
- Supplier's address and named contact details, including phone, fax and e-mail.
- Type of subscription – eg membership subscription, print package, print plus electronic journal package. If the journal comes as part of a package, all related titles must be indicated, as this can help to avoid problems when individual titles come up for cancellation.

- Frequency – eg daily, weekly, monthly, annually.
- Number of copies subscribed to – if these are for separate buildings, 'bill to' and 'deliver to' instructions should be recorded.
- Subscription period – always include month as well as year as some subscriptions will straddle two financial years.
- Anticipated renewal date – as above, always include month and year of renewal.
- Subscription costs – amount paid, date paid, unit of currency, plus invoice date and number.
- Number of claims generated – per title, per publisher and per agent.
- Fund codes to be debited – this may be a simple code such as 'serials', 'standing orders', etc. However, allocation can be broken down to a more detailed level to reflect departmental or even individual interests. The latter is particularly useful when academic staff or researchers leave or retire, as it is possible to produce lists of titles in which they had expressed interest which it may be desirable to cancel. Also, as there is an increasing interest in establishing the costs of library support for particular research projects or teaching programmes, any data which links specific journals to programmes or courses of study should be recorded.

It is also important to record any exceptional expenditure relating to individual titles, for example, costs for additional volumes, supplements and back issues. Provided there are sufficient local fields available in each record, the golden rule should always be that if you think the information might be useful at a later date – record it now!

Financial reports

If you have specified your initial management information profile correctly, it should be possible to respond to the requirements of library managers for financial data on serial expenditure. Virtually the only thing you can guarantee about financial reports is that you are unlikely to require precisely the same data in the same format twice in succession, and the production of one report invariably leads to another.

Financial reports serve a variety of different functions. They are primarily required to justify funding decisions and inform future budget plans. In academic libraries, they are increasingly required for quality assessment visits, where it may be necessary to provide details of expenditure on print, electronic serials and CD-ROMs to support a particular discipline. It is also helpful to include information on the average cost of material in the specific subject area under review and to compare this with serials prices in general. Reports are also required to inform collection development decisions, for example, an academic library may wish to carry out a serials expenditure analysis by subject area both before and after the results of an RAE are known, or when the parent institution's latest strategic plan is issued. In these cases, the library wants to ensure that the largest consumers of serials resources are appropriately aligned to current institutional priorities. Financial reports can also be used as an aid to collection weeding. For example, if savings in serials expenditure are required, libraries may choose to target high cost–low use titles as a first priority.

In recent years, one of the most frequently asked-for reports is expenditure by publisher. Demand has largely been driven by the need to respond to or assess the various publisher deals for electronic journals, although the standard requirements of monitoring publisher price rises and their share of total library expenditure remain constant. It is also important to remember that in any given financial year, you could be processing invoices from the immediate previous year, current year, and immediate following year. Thus financial reports need to be able to distinguish between total amount spent in the institutional fiscal year (which could relate to more than one subscription year) and total expenditure in a subscription year.

When planning for an upgrade to or a replacement for an existing serials management system, it is essential to sit down and consider in detail the number, type and frequency of any financial reports you are likely to require, including the data fields that are necessary for each one. As a minimum, you should be able to produce:

- total serials expenditure per financial year/per subscription year
- total outstanding serials commitment per financial year/subscription year
- total expenditure by format – eg printed journals, electronic journals, CD-ROMs, standing orders, official publications
- total expenditure by source of supply
- annual percentage price rise, in total, by format and by publisher
- total expenditure by fund code – eg cost centre, department, special account number
- total expenditure by publisher, currency or country of origin
- expenditure estimates for next year, based on inflation patterns of previous year(s).

Up-to-date, flexible and accurate expenditure reports are an essential library management tool, and they are becoming increasingly important in a climate where IT is facilitating greater end-user access to serials literature than ever before. As more journals become available electronically from the users' desktops, they may increasingly question why the resources need to be handled centrally. Librarians can add value to this information resource by negotiating favourable licence terms, evaluating different information providers, and building effective OPAC links and subject access routes.

As this chapter has shown, budgeting ordering and paying for serials is far from straightforward, and serials librarians should be able to continue to demonstrate that they provide the best means of managing and delivering a high quality journals service in the hybrid library environment.

References

Association of Research Libraries (1999) *Monograph and serial costs in ARL libraries, 1986–1998*, available at:
http://www.arl.org/stats/arlstat/1998t2.html

Astle, D and Hamaker, C (1986) Pricing by geography: British journal pricing 1986, including developments in other countries, *Library Acquisitions: Practice & Theory*, **10**, 165–81.

Blackwell's Information Services (1990–9) *Periodicals price index, British libraries*.

Cox, J (1998) The changing economic model of scholarly publishing: uncertainty, complexity and multi-media serials, *INSPEL: International Journal of Special Libraries*, **32** (2), 69–78, available at:
http://forge.fh-potsdam.de/~IFLA/INSPEL/cont322.htm

Duff, K E (1999) Scholarly societies: pricing models for online journals, *Against the Grain*, **11** (1), 23–4.

Fishwick, F (1986) The effects of unstable exchange rates on the prices of books and journals. In *Serials '86: proceedings of the UK Serials Group Conference*, UKSG.

Harnad, S (1995) Electronic scholarly publication, *Serials Review*, **21** (1), 78–80.

Hitchcock, S, Carr, L and Hall, W (1997) Web journals publishing: a UK perspective, *Serials*, **10** (3), 285–99, available at:
http://journals.ecs.soton.ac.uk/uksg.htm

Hobohm, H-C (1997) Changing the galaxy: on the transformation of a printed journal to the Internet, *First Monday*, **2** (11), available at:
http://www.firstmonday.dk/issues/issue2_11/hobohm/index.html

Houbeck, R L (1986) British journal pricing: Enigma Variations, or what will the US market bear? *Library Acquisitions: Practice & Theory*, **10**, 183–97.

Hutchins, J (1997) Developing a formula for library resource funding. In Baker, D (ed) *Resource management in academic libraries*, Library Association Publishing.

LIBLICENSE: licensing digital information, a resource for librarians
http://www.library.yale.edu/~llicense/index.shtml

Library and Information Statistics Unit (1998) *1998 Library & information statistics tables for the United Kingdom*, Loughborough University, available at:
http://info.lboro.ac.uk/department/dils/lisu/list98/speclib.html

http://info.lboro.ac.uk/department/dils/lisu/list98/acad.html

Loughner, W (1999) Top ten science publishers take 76 percent of science budget, *Newsletter on Serials Pricing Issues*, 221 (20 May), available at:
http://www.lib.unc.edu/prices/1999/PRIC221.HTML

Martin, M S (1980) Allocation of money within the book budget, *Foundations in Library & Information Science*, **10** (1).

McCabe, M J (1999) *Academic journal pricing and market power: a portfolio approach*, available at:
http://www.econ.gatech.edu/~mmccabe/journalWEA.pdf

Naylor, B (1995) The future of the scholarly journal. In Okerson, A S and O'Donnell, J J (eds) *Scholarly journals at the crossroads: a subversive proposal for electronic publishing*, Office of Scientific and Academic Publishing, Association of Research Libraries, available at:
http://www.arl.org/scomm/subversive/sub11.html

Newsletter on Serials Pricing Issues
http://www.lib.unc.edu/prices/about.html

Nisonger, T E (1998) *Management of serials in libraries*, Libraries Unlimited.

Odlyzko, A (1997) The economics of electronic journals, *First Monday*, **2** (8), available at:
http://www.firstmonday.dk/issues/issue2_8/odlyzko

SCONUL (1993) *Annual statistics, 1991–92*.

SCONUL (1999) *Annual library statistics, 1997–98*.

Ulrich's international periodicals directory, 1973, Bowker.

Ulrich's international periodicals directory, 1999, Bowker.

Woodward, H (1990) Financial control and budgeting. In Graham, M and Tipple, F (eds) *Serials management: a practical handbook*, Aslib.

5

The acquisition of serials

Tony Kidd and Albert Prior

Introduction

The previous chapter considered the factors that surround journal purchasing decisions. This chapter looks at what happens once the decision to purchase has been made, in particular how the journal is acquired. Most print and many electronic journals are acquired via subscription agents, and they are our primary focus, although there is some discussion towards the end of the chapter on acquisition of print journals from other sources, including by gift or exchange. In this arena, as in so many others, however, the advent of the electronic journal has complicated matters, and the subscription agent now has a number of actual or potential competitors. But we shall begin with an examination of the work of the 'traditional' agent.

Subscription agents

Why do subscription agents exist? What services do they provide which cannot be undertaken by libraries themselves? Which types of libraries use them? What is their relationship with publishers? In order to establish why the subscription agent came into being, it is worth reminding ourselves very briefly of the rôle of two other key players in the communication chain: the publisher and the library.

Publishers are responsible for taking written manuscripts from authors, subjecting them to a rigorous refereeing process, undertaking a wide variety of other editorial, marketing and production functions that make up the publishing process, and delivering the journal as we know it. This process of refining, undertaking peer review and quality control, and providing a means for the dissemination of information is the rôle of the publisher. There are many thousands of publishers of scholarly and research material around the world. Chapter 2 gives more information on the publisher's rôle.

The library acts as a centralized purchasing department and resource or depository, for its parent organization, providing a support to the organization's research or teaching activities. It acts as a single point where current journals can be accessed and back-runs stored, offering cost-effective access for a large number of people along with a guarantee of safe storage. A major academic research library could subscribe to as many as 10,000 current journals. Library staff will also assist access to information, and educate the library's customers in information use and management.

Subscription agents are the third component of this supporting cast in the communication chain: the single point between the thousands of publishers and thousands of libraries that support research output. They are uniquely placed between the two, responding to their respective requirements, and developing products, services and procedures designed to improve the speed and efficiency of this complex process.

The overall aim of these three partners is to facilitate the process of publishing and the dissemination of the results of research undertaken by scholars or scientists. The author and user communities are key players at the beginning and end of the information process, often of course one and the same community. The arrival of the Internet has sometimes brought with it the view that this new technological phenomenon will enable scholars to communicate the results of research amongst each other without the need for publishers, libraries or intermediaries of any sort. Whilst this will undoubtedly happen on some scale, there are equally those who emphasize that the need for organizations such as those described above is even more great in a world where there is increasing information, in a variety of formats and often made available in an unstructured way.

Libraries use agents therefore to make life easier for them, in the area of journal acquisitions, whether print or electronic. Agents act as specialists that support libraries in this area of library administration, enabling libraries to keep processing staff to the minimum and to concentrate resources on user service functions.

Agents' services are paid for through a combination of discounts on the prices of journal titles they purchase from publishers and service charges made to their customers, both representing the added value that the agent provides to these two groups.

Scale of journals purchasing

What is the scale of journals publishing and library subscriptions? It is estimated that the market worldwide for journals published in the UK is close to £400 million, of which a little over 70% is export sales. Global journals purchasing by libraries is large. The value of institutional journal subscriptions worldwide was estimated some years ago to be in the region of £1.8 billion. This is predominantly buying by academic and research libraries, the main customers of subscription agents. Total spending on books and journals by UK university libraries is around £100 million, with journals comprising nearly 60% of this (Davies, 1999). The large majority of libraries choose to purchase journals via subscription agents to benefit from the efficiencies they offer and to avoid the massive administrative overhead which direct purchasing would involve.

A leading subscription agent would expect to be dealing with some 40,000 publishers, and maintain a subscriptions database containing anything up to 200,000 titles. The ISSN International Centre in Paris, responsible for coordinating national centres that assign ISSN serial identifiers in each country, eg the British Library's ISSN UK Centre, or the Library of Congress's National Serials Data Program, has some 890,000 serials title records available through *ISSN Online* (also available on CD-ROM). Publishers vary tremendously in size ranging from the major international commercial science/technology/medicine (STM) publishers such as Elsevier Science, Kluwer Academic, Springer Verlag and Academic Press, which publish hundreds of titles each, down to the specialist society publishers with perhaps one or two serial publications. A title from a small specialist publisher may be as much in demand from a research library as a journal from a leading commercial publisher, depending on the research and information needs of the library. It is true to say, however, that the 80/20 rule probably applies in journal publishing – a relatively small group of publishers makes up the bulk of the value of subscription agents' purchases. The predominant countries of publication of scholarly journals are the USA, the UK, the Netherlands, Germany and France. Agents handle serials of all types – journals, periodicals, magazines – in print, as well as in other formats such as microform, CD-ROMs, diskettes, tape, online and now Internet-based publications.

Library purchasing

Libraries similarly vary considerably in their nature, size and journal requirements. A major university research library may subscribe to thousands of journal titles published around the world, and have an ongoing need for this core set of publications, whilst the numbers of titles taken by a medium-sized library in a pharmaceutical company could be 600–800. The titles taken by this pharmaceutical library would be reviewed annually and the list modified at each subscription renewal in order to meet the company's changing research needs. The service demands made on the subscription agent by such a library may differ considerably to those required by, say, a society or university library. The rôles of libraries are also changing as the Internet has an increasing impact on how research information is published and made available. Often the library will no longer own the information it pays for but rather be licensed to access it through the subscription. Readers may visit the library less and less to refer to the publications purchased, but increasingly expect to access the data at their desktops. These issues have an impact also on the way in which libraries acquire materials and their relationship with their agents or suppliers.

It is not just the large numbers involved that make scholarly communication a complicated process. It is the fact that constant variation is one of the ingredients: journal titles change, or they are acquired by other publishers. Their format may change, as may their frequency. Publishers move and so address changes have to be made. Prices alter each year and are subject to fluctuations in international exchange rates. Today, these complications are increased as the Internet and the web have an ever increasing influence on the way in which journals are published, bringing the need for new systems and procedures, and highlighting issues such as licensing, access arrangements, different formats and archiving. Similarly, within the library community, changes are taking place in the methods of purchasing as increasingly libraries work within consortia to achieve cost savings and the sharing of resources.

Who are the agents?

Before going on to consider the work of the subscription agent, it is worth establishing exactly to whom we are referring in this chapter.

The Association of Subscription Agents (ASA), which is based in the UK but is an international body, has some 40 members. Many of these provide a service within their own country or region, but there is a small number of major international subscription agents, providing a global service from offices around the world, which are significantly larger than the other agents.

In recent years, the total number of subscription agents has declined, and there has been a tendency towards a concentration of business amongst the major companies. Faced with declining operating margins, and the need for extensive investment for new systems or the development of the new electronic products that are increasingly sought by library customers, some smaller agents have either discontinued business or been acquired by a competitor. In 1999, this process was emphasized by the announcement of the proposed joint venture between Swets Subscription Service and Blackwell's Information Services, by the acquisition by Ebsco of the German Lange & Springer agency, and by the takeover of the subscription agency interests of Dawson by RoweCom from the USA (Merging subscription agents, 1999). Nevertheless, the ASA is in fact currently growing, as a result of a membership push throughout the world and the recent successful appointment of a paid Secretary General to represent the Association's interests – a current list of members is available at its website. It has recently introduced an associate member category to allow other intermediaries, with an interest in serials, to participate. In addition it has held discussions with EIDA, the Electronic Information Distributors Association, with a view to their members joining the ASA.

The ASA issues Guidelines (ASA, 1999), recently revised, that indicate that the members exist 'to achieve the highest standards of service for both customers and publishers, and to improve relationships and terms with publishers.' The Association's aim is to foster the use of a 'best practice' approach to customer and publisher service and to represent members' common interests, whilst recognizing that agents are in competition with each other. Under its comprehensive list of services for libraries it includes the following that members should undertake:

- maintain up-to-date journal and price information
- keep information on the availability and prices of electronic journals and provide advice on their licensing and access
- provide clear, detailed invoices noting customers' special requirements
- process and order efficiently new subscriptions
- renew subscriptions in good time
- respond effectively to claims for missing issues.

At its meetings it addresses a range of topics of common interest to members, such as VAT/sales taxes, general relationships with publishers, trends in journal subscriptions, standards for electronic data interchange (EDI) in serials, trends in library purchasing, etc. It also runs an annual conference, attended not only by agents but also for the benefit of publishers and libraries, and is exploring other events and activities. The theme of the 2000 conference was 'Consortia Purchasing – the next ten years', with implications for managers of consortia, librarians, publishers, intermediaries and subscription agents.

Changing rôle of the agent

The role of the subscription agent is changing, however, as increasing numbers of journal titles are now published electronically and publishers introduce new business models for pricing and selling their content. Many of the agents have anticipated these changes in recent years, by developing services beyond the traditional ones – offering online access to their databases, providing electronic tables of contents of research journals, and enabling Internet access to titles traditionally delivered on CD-ROM. Nevertheless for many of the smaller agents it is a testing time as they review their strategies to meet the changing needs of their customers and develop the systems to handle the new formats and pricing options of journals. The new electronic environment brings with it many opportunities for the enterprising and agile agent, but threats for those who are not able to adapt and develop new services for new requirements.

Already a number of the major agents provide their customers with gateway services to a range of publishers' electronic journals, offering users functions such as a single interface and searching, browsing and alerting of relevant information, along with facilities to help library managers, such as usage data. They have also become proficient in assisting their customers in handling the licences that are part and parcel of electronic journal publishing. The growth of library consortia around the world has also been a particular area of attention for agents in their rôle as an intermediary between publishers and libraries, and this will be covered later in this chapter, for both print and electronic journals.

Electronic publishing has brought with it the arrival of new service companies and organizations to meet the changing needs of publishers and end-users in the area of full-text electronic journals. Some provide electronic journals services for and on behalf of a range of publishers. These, along with the agents, fall into a category often referred to as intermediaries and aggregators and include companies such as ingenta, CatchWord, Cadmus, etc. Existing intermediaries, such as secondary publishers and database hosts, also increasingly offer libraries and researchers access to electronic journal collections. Whilst some of these exist to help publishers in their Internet publishing activities, others may be seen by some of the agents as competitors in the provision of gateways or single interfaces to electronic publications. In fact, however, it is apparent that each of these different types of intermediary has a different rôle to play, and different added value to bring, in the information chain, and therefore the rôle of the subscription agent is not considered to be one that is necessarily under serious threat.

Agents' services

As we have already established, the business of the subscription agent is to provide a service, or a range of services, to the communities that it serves: traditionally publishers and libraries. Whilst there has been debate over the years as to whom the agent is really representing (a more pressing question nowadays in the world of consortia and negotiation services), any overview of the nature and extent of the work performed by agents reveals that an agent doing its job well will be of great service to both of the other parties.

Whilst most of this section will be devoted to the traditional and more recent electronic services that agents offer libraries and scholars, it is important to spend some time considering the publisher–agent relationship and what the latter can offer.

For publishers

The publisher–agent relationship is just as important as that established between the agent and the library, and the regular contact and communication that takes place will almost inevitably result in a better service to subscribers.

For many years, agents have been a source of market intelligence for publishers, reporting back on trends within libraries such as budgetary developments and cancellation rates. They have also been able to offer marketing services including promoting new titles via their catalogues and information bulletins, providing targeted addresses for mailings, and notifying subscribers of changes to journal titles and frequencies.

More than anything else, agents offer publishers the economies and efficiencies that come with dealing with a handful of organizations for the vast majority of their subscriptions rather than having to deal with many thousands of individual libraries. In simple terms, this means:

* a guarantee of major payments made in a timely fashion rather than many smaller payments spread across a wider period of time
* consolidated renewal listings sent in bulk and often in electronic form
* dissemination of new pricing information to all subscribers.

In less tangible terms, agents also offer a customer service layer between the publisher and the library, which can often serve to diffuse difficult situations and problems.

Very tangible evidence of successful cooperation between publishers and agents is the work of ICEDIS (International Committee for EDI for Serials) (Summers, 1995; Benjamin, 1999), which over several years has sought to use EDI to improve the quality, speed and efficiency of data interchange between the two parties.

Traditional services to libraries

Controlling the renewal process

The subscription agent coordinates and manages the whole renewal process on behalf of libraries by providing a listing of all the active titles currently subscribed to, together with their expiry dates. Such a listing, generally provided in June or July each year, gives libraries an opportunity to consider their holdings, to consult with academic departments or researchers, and to make any changes before the new subscription year commences. To allow renewals to proceed smoothly, most agents ask libraries to renew or cancel titles by the end of September at the latest. Libraries can maintain one central record of all their subscriptions, and are protected from the mass of renewal reminders that they would receive if the subscriptions were placed directly with individual publishers. Renewal control – preventing subscriptions from expiring and ensuring they are renewed on time – is one of the key functions of the subscription agent.

Financial management

For most research libraries, journal subscriptions will account for the largest part of the acquisitions budget. The nature of the industry is such that subscriptions have to be paid for in advance and that they are subject not only to inflation on the cover price of the journal but to fluctuations in exchange rates.

Subscription agents assist libraries in a variety of ways in this area. Almost as soon as publishers have announced their subscription rates for the forthcoming year, agents will have entered them onto their own databases, enabling them to provide forecasts of likely price inflation as well as providing libraries with listings of their own titles reflecting the new prices. Some agents provide price analysis reports based on country of publication and subject area, and these are generally available on request or from their websites.

Consolidated invoicing, in the preferred currency of the library, is another feature of the agent's service, making invoices easier and cheaper to verify, process and pay. A number of agents offer pre-payment plans whereby libraries can receive small discounts for making a bulk payment without itemized prices in advance of the new subscription year. A reconciliation invoice, with itemized prices, is provided at an agreed time.

Invoices from subscription agents can be split by fund or budget codes to allow for devolved budgeting or cost recovery, and they are now available in machine-readable form for use with spreadsheet packages or the serials modules of automated library management systems.

Bibliographical control

Serials management and control is a complex business, and mistakes made in the areas of renewals or financial management can be costly in service and monetary terms. Adding to this complexity is the fact that the bibliographical data surrounding subscriptions is constantly changing. Titles are sold and acquired by other publishers, formats, frequencies and titles change, and prices rarely stay static. The arrival of electronic versions of the print journal further complicates the picture, with differential pricing, separate ISSNs and a myriad of access options.

Subscription agents, through their close contact with publishers, are able to maintain a high level of control over this constantly changing data, and in doing so, make it available to libraries on a regular basis by way of regular information reports and bulletins. The major agents make available to their customers an annual catalogue of the most popular titles on their database.

Claims management

Handling claims for missing issues is a major exercise for any library that subscribes to a large collection of journals. Although, over the years, automated systems have refined this process, it is still time-consuming and problematic.

In addition to providing a central point to which to send claims for missing issues, as well as their filtering and ultimate resolution, agents help libraries in a variety of other ways. Through their representation on SISAC (Serials Industry Systems Advisory Committee), agents have worked with the major library systems vendors in producing standards for generating and sending claims using EDI. They have also helped libraries through the automation process by providing feedback and data on the timeliness of computer-generated claims.

Journals consolidation

Consolidation is a form of outsourcing that is becoming increasingly popular with libraries of all types. It is a departure from the traditional method of delivery in that the agent receives issues on behalf of the library in the first instance. At the most basic level, these are checked in and delivered to the library with a consignment listing. Any shortfall is claimed. Some agents will also offer a variety of processing tasks including date stamping, creating and attaching circulation lists, affixing security triggers and ownership or class mark stamping. Libraries use consolidation services for a variety of reasons and generally offset the additional charges against the benefits to the service they can offer their users.

Other value-added services

Subscription agents hold a vast amount of information and expertise, and offer far more than has been briefly outlined above. In addition to a single point of contact and communication for all subscription-related matters, they can provide sample copies, basic claim and order forms, and subject listings based on their considerable databases of titles. A number of agents also maintain specialist departments for the supply of complete volumes of backsets of journals.

Electronic services to libraries

Online access

For over 15 years, agents have been making their proprietary data available to customers via online services. In doing so, they have enabled libraries to undertake bibliographical checking, place orders and claims electronically and review their holdings. Originally available as dial-up services, most of these have migrated to the world wide web and are generally available to customers at no additional charge.

Serials management systems

Mention has already been made of the complexity of journals. Creating automated routines for the check-in and claiming of journals has proved to be just as complicated, and most of the early serials modules offered by the integrated systems vendors proved to be weak or undeveloped. In the early 1980s, subscription agents began developing their own standalone serials packages, based on their extensive experience and knowledge of this publication type. Although systems suppliers' serials modules have improved over recent years, agents' modules are still often more sophisticated. However, many libraries will prefer the advantages of integration with catalogue, acquisition and circulation modules now more readily available from the standard system suppliers.

CD-ROM and database services

Agents have handled subscriptions to CD-ROM databases for a number of years now. Many libraries are content for them to be included in their general journal subscriptions handling, and agents have developed an expertise in dealing with the licensing issues that accompany this format.

More recently, the content of these databases has become accessible over the Internet, removing some of the local storage and maintenance problems that libraries previously faced with local networking. Subscription agents have moved quickly into this area and, working closely with data providers, have installed servers in their offices onto which they will load databases that customers require for trial or real use, providing access in addition to the subscription administration.

Current awareness services

With the introduction of the so-called ETOC (electronic table of contents) services in the early 1990s, subscription agents moved into the area of content creation, maintenance and distribution for the first time. The introduction of these services coincided with a growing move towards an access rather than a holdings strategy in many research libraries, and they flourished quite rapidly, with anything between 10,000 and 30,000 titles being included.

Today, they provide agents' customers with current awareness information as well as growing databases for search and retrieval. The data is generally made available in batch format for use by libraries in their own local systems, on CD-ROM or increasingly via the web. Document delivery modules, usually in association with commercial or established document supply organizations, have supported a number of these services.

Electronic journals

Electronic journals are covered in greater detail below, but it is no exaggeration to say that they present subscription agents with their biggest challenge to date, not only in terms of how they are managed, but also through their impact on the long-term viability of their traditional services. Agents have taken a number of positive steps to protect their own business and to support their customers in this most difficult period of transition. All agents involved in this area accept that there is still much work to be done and investment to be made, before they can claim to have guaranteed their position in the electronic scholarly communication chain.

Consortia purchasing

So far in this chapter, we have described some of the traditional services provided by serials agents, together with examples of some of the more recent service enhancements enabled through electronic access. The description has been in the context of a single library obtaining its periodical requirements through an agent, but we now move on to consider the development of library consortia, and their influence on the acquisition of serials.

At least in the UK, consortia, and the formal tendering procedures that are normally employed by them, have not been much in evidence until fairly recently. In all sectors, normal practice was to rely on local and/or well-established suppliers, with individual, and perhaps not always very intense, negotiation on terms. Several factors, some specific to the UK, others more widely applicable, have changed this behaviour in recent years:

1   The continuing restrictions on library expenditure, coupled with continuing severe inflation in journal prices, discussed in Chapter 4, force library budget controllers to seek savings wherever possible. The serials budget, consuming well over half the materials budget in many university libraries (and in many commercial and health sector libraries), is an obvious, probably *the* obvious, place to look.

2   Cooperation is more widely accepted, established, welcomed, and sometimes enforced, than ever before. In the higher education (HE) sector, the Follett Report (Joint Funding Councils' Libraries Review Group, 1993) on the future development of libraries, and the Anderson Report (Joint Funding Councils' Libraries Review Group, 1995) on research support, have both established a climate of working together. The National Health Service (NHS) regions have also begun to cooperate more closely, as symbolized by the establishment of the national post of NHS Library Adviser in 1995.

3   European Union legislation enforces tendering in the public sector, for all substantial contracts, ie those totalling more than 200,000 Euro (at present exchange rates, around £130,000) (Council of the European Communities, 1992). When this directive was published, there were suggestions that it did not apply to the purchase of journals (or books) for libraries, as the value of an order for even the most expensive single title is below the threshold. It is generally accepted now that the total value of the contract is the determining factor. While compulsory tendering does not in itself enforce the formation of consortia, the costs and administration of tendering encourage this process, and it is likely that a better deal will be available for larger levels of business put out to tender.

4   In the HE sector, regional purchasing consortia have been formed by groups of universities. These purchasing groups concerned themselves initially with commodities such as stationery, catering supplies, etc, but have now extended their interest to most areas of university purchasing, including libraries. Once one consortium won improvements in terms as a result of going out to tender, it became apparent that university libraries in areas not tendering would be almost bound to be disadvantaged, and most UK areas have now followed suit.

One of the pioneers in university consortia tendering in the UK was the Southern Universities Purchasing Consortium (SUPC), including over 30 higher education institutions, ranging geographically from Plymouth to East Anglia. Their serials contract commenced in the mid 1990s (Ball and Wright, 1997), and, as is typical, runs for three years with an extension option for a further two years. The Northern Ireland university libraries entered into an even earlier consortium arrangement in the early 1990s (Lyttle and Shorley, 1994). Although the consortium was set up with assistance from university purchasing staff, the initiative in this case came from the libraries. Over the UK, there are further examples of library consortia, divided between those based on the broader university purchasing groups, and those based on library groupings, such as SCURL (Scottish Confederation of University and Research Libraries), NEYAL (North East and Yorkshire Academic Libraries) and CALIM (Consortium of Academic Libraries in Manchester). This distinction is, in practice, of limited importance. In all cases, both purchasing and library professional staff take part in the process, the effectiveness of which depends on the close cooperation between the two groups, both employing their particular professional skills.

In passing, it should be said that many of these consortia have moved on, or are moving on, to ask for bids for the supply of books and standing orders, but that is outside the scope of this volume.

Beyond HE, the NHS is, at the time of writing, moving towards going out to tender for the supply of serials for all hospital libraries in England and Wales (Pye and Ball, 1999, 144). Various groups of government libraries have also gone out to tender (see eg Snowley, 1995). Public libraries are participating more in consortia, but mainly for book supply, as their periodical requirements are, in comparison, minor. It is more problematic (and perhaps would be illegal) for commercial companies to combine for this purpose, but there have been moves, in for example the information-intensive pharmaceutical industry, to centralize a multinational company's library purchases (Brown, 1999). This can be particularly appropriate for serials, published internationally, and serviced by agents with offices in many different countries. It may be especially useful, but also especially complex to negotiate, as a means of providing *electronic* access to serials for a company's laboratories and offices throughout the world.

Are consortia an appropriate means of acquiring serial publications? For the reasons given at the start of this section, they are almost certainly here to stay, and indeed likely to grow in importance. They have introduced a greater professionalism into relations between libraries and agents, and have not significantly reduced an individual library's influence on purchasing, providing of course that consortium participants are consulted at all stages of the tender process, and have a voice in the final decisions that are made. Once a contract has been awarded, to one or more agents, it is incumbent upon the consortium members to honour that contract, and to switch subscriptions if appropriate.

For agents, consortia are both an opportunity and a threat. The opportunity is there to win a substantially larger volume of business. The consortium tendering process also encourages agents to monitor constantly the efficiency and effectiveness of their operations. This is necessary, first, to support the provision of terms financially attractive enough to win the contract initially. Secondly, Service Level Agreements, or Statements of Service Standards, are a regular feature of most contracts, including meetings annually or twice a year between the consortium and the agent to review performance against stated targets. A potential threat is market instability, arising from the relatively small number of large agents and the possible destabilizing effects of moving large numbers of subscriptions if a contract is not renewed, especially if several contracts come up for renewal at a similar time. The SUPC universities, for example, spend around £12.5 million per annum on serials (Pye and Ball, 1999, 79), though not all this expenditure necessarily goes through consortium agreements. This is unlikely to be a problem globally for the large international agents, but could seriously affect operations in a particular country – and conceivably raise monopoly problems for libraries, if the number of large agents is reduced yet further.

Assuming the continued existence of consortia, what are the practical considerations for serials staff taking part in the tendering process? There is not space to go into detail here, and articles cited earlier (Ball and Wright, 1997; Lyttle and Shorley, 1994; Snowley, 1995; plus Taylor-Roe, 1997) provide more information. However, certain points should be mentioned:

1   The various legal requirements for EU tendering, relating to publication in the *Official Journal*, timetable matters, valid decision-making criteria, feedback to unsuccessful tenderers, etc, must be understood and followed. There will be similar rules in other state or federal jurisdictions. Purchasing professionals will be able to provide expert guidance in this field.

2   The Invitation To Tender (ITT) document is critical. If possible, obtain advice from other consortia. There are tentative moves towards standardizing such ITTs, likely to be welcomed both by agents and libraries, although scope for variation will still be necessary. Criteria both for shortlisting, and for final selection, must be discussed and decided on well in advance, together with approximate weightings, although details will become clearer as the process, which is likely to take at least several months, develops.

3   For shortlisting, in addition to pricing offers, and service responses to the ITT, financial analysis of tendering companies is vital. Purchasing staff can again advise on undertaking this.

4 References from other library customers are important, though most authoritative if based on sound analysis rather than anecdotal evidence, and from libraries of a similar size and type, with a reasonable level of business with the agent, and with a reasonable length of experience.

5 Visits to the shortlisted agents can be most informative, to gain an impression of the service 'on the ground', and to judge the competence, dynamism, and innovation potential of the company management.

6 It is important that the final decision is not based solely on discount offered. Because of the competitive nature of the industry, it is unlikely that discounts available will either be very different from what the library already receives, or that the packages offered by the leading contenders will vary dramatically. Service issues are also important. To give but one example, the Scottish university libraries used the following weightings to reach their final decision:
  • pricing factors 35%
  • response to ITT/service factors 21%
  • visits to shortlisted agents 19%
  • references 12.5%
  • monitoring by existing Scottish customers 12.5%.

7 After the award of a contract, it is essential that arrangements are in place to monitor performance, by both the libraries and the agent, and that regular meetings are held to discuss and improve performance.

Electronic journals

The origins of electronic journals, their advantages and disadvantages, and technical developments, have all been discussed in Chapters 1 and 2. This chapter is concerned with their *acquisition*. The very concept of acquisition in this context is debatable, for various reasons. Does a library 'acquire' an electronic journal mounted on a publisher's server, or the server of some intermediary? Will the 'subscription' model itself persist (see Chapter 3)? The discussion at this point, however, will concentrate on 'subscriptions' to 'journals', and, in the main, to commercially published journals. These are likely to persist for some time to come, while supplemented by several other models of access to the research article, the basic information unit from which journals are assembled. The debate on how, or even whether, commercial publishers will continue to exist, is covered in Chapter 2.

Although most analysis in this book is subject to rapid change, the acquisition of electronic journals, with its associated problems, is going through a particularly delicate stage, in the UK and throughout the world. Experiments have been around for a decade or more. The first successful electronic journals, such as Steven Harnad's *Psycoloquy*, John Unsworth's *Postmodern Culture* (Amiran and Unsworth, 1991), and James O'Donnell's *Bryn Mawr Classical Review* (O'Donnell, 1996), date from around 1990. But it was not until the triumph of the Internet and the world wide web that existing commercial publishers began to take much notice of the new possibilities, and not until the last two or three years that most STM publishers, and a significant number of social sciences and humanities publishers, have begun to provide full electronic access to their journals.

Pricing

A consequence of this novelty, and of the flexibility and new opportunities offered by electronic journals, is that there is no single recognized commercial model for pricing acquisition of, or access to, electronic journals. For print journals, there is usually a straightforward annual subscription, although there are occasional possibilities of a combined price for several titles bought together, or a cheaper annual rate if two or three years are paid for at once, and there is very often a considerable price differential between an institutional and an individual subscription. Pricing for an electronic journal is rarely as simple, and the first challenge is to discover what price options are available. Agents have put great efforts in very recent years into extending the information supplied through their bibliographic databases, described above, but these databases cannot sometimes cope with all the options available.

Science, for example, has a range of possible subscription prices, from that for an individual member of the American Association for the Advancement of Science, to the price for sitewide access for all members of a large university (based on staff plus student FTE numbers), including an option allowing an institution to buy access for individual terminals in a library, itself not a straightforward proposition where institutions insist that all network traffic goes through a local, or even a national, cache. A further interesting option is to allow access from one PC to *Science* for 24 hours for $10 (Spinella, 1999). The American Chemical Society offers different rates to institutions prepared to limit access to a certain number of Class C IP machine address ranges (American Chemical Society, 1999). These are just examples. Other publishers insist on individual negotiation to reach a price for institutional access.

Among the variables that can influence the price charged by the publisher are the numbers of:

- students and/or staff (or researchers)
- sites or buildings to be given access (with complex definitions of what constitutes a separate 'site' or a separate 'building')

- networked machines
- simultaneous accesses by users
- Class B or Class C IP address ranges.

It is apparent that the serials librarian is faced with a very complex decision making process.

Although there can be a structure of different prices offered, the initial building block price for electronic access is usually based on the print subscription. Publishers are still feeling their way in this area, and usually try to link an electronic to a print subscription. A recent survey of publishers' 1999 pricing policies (Prior, 1999) reveals that 62% have a single 'print plus online' price, indicating that electronic access is 'bundled in' with the print subscription. Where a surcharge is levied, with separate options of 'print' and 'print plus online', it varies from 8% to 65%, with the most popular being around 15–20%. Around half of the publishers surveyed now offer a separate 'online' subscription, at 65–150% of the print price, with 90–100% most common. Until very recently, publishers have been wary of providing this option, concerned about the effect on their print sales. Librarians have argued for this choice, to give greater flexibility, although it has to be said that relatively few 'online only' subscriptions have yet been taken out. This is likely to change in the next few years, as discussed elsewhere in this book. Perhaps the most revealing statistic from Prior's survey is that 30% of publishers have altered their pricing policy this year. This is a strong indication that the market has yet to settle, and that the figures given above may well look very different before very long.

Availability

Electronic journals are available from a wide variety of sources. First, they can be acquired individually via the serials agent, in the same way as print journals. However, because electronic journals are still in their infancy, acquisition is not straightforward, even after the satisfactory resolution of the pricing questions discussed above. After payment, most publishers require libraries to register in some way to gain access to the article full text held on the publishers' websites; security considerations demand restriction, usually either by IP address, or by user name/password. Registration can be problematic, for example it can demand the input of a customer number, often unknown by the library (as it is a number referring to the transaction between the publisher and the agent). This can become more complicated, when the (print) serial is acquired via the agent's consolidation service (and online availability is linked to the print subscription), and the publisher may not initially even be aware that a particular university library is entitled to electronic access.

It is to be hoped that many of these difficulties are transitional, and will seem quaint and old-fashioned to someone reading this book in a few years. At present, however, they can be very time-consuming and frustrating restrictions on providing quick access to journal content. One possible solution, in this age of 'disintermediation', is to order journals direct from the publisher. While there is certainly much more direct contact between publishers and librarians in the age of the electronic journal – and this is to be welcomed – it would appear to be a retrograde step to return to very many individual financial transactions between publisher and library, the very situation that serials agents were set up to alleviate.

The large serials agents have themselves each developed their own electronic journal management system, to try to overcome some of the access problems, and to preserve their rôle, and financial health, in the new era. These systems (eg *Blackwells Electronic Journal Navigator*, *EBSCO Online*, RoweCom's *Information Quest*, and *SwetsNet*) provide, for a relatively modest additional charge, a standard 'front-end' access to many publishers' journals – one of the standard complaints concerning electronic journals is the variety of formats in which they are presented. If required, a standard user name/password will gain entry to all eligible journals, reducing the problem of user name overload. The systems will also provide management and usage information – see Chapter 8 below.

Electronic journals are also mounted by a number of other intermediaries. A variety of companies, specialists in providing access to databases, have recently extended their portfolios to include electronic journals, often linked to their databases, eg Ovid and Bell & Howell. In other words, if a researcher finds a reference on a particular database, it may be that the full text of the article can be immediately available. Subscriptions to these electronic journals are generally sold in bundles, perhaps by subject groupings, with business and medicine probably the two most popular fields. Some suppliers offer the opportunity to substitute titles. The long-established OCLC provides Electronic Collections Online, a similar system, with particular emphasis on the continuing availability of journal archives, at a relatively small cost, even after a subscription has been cancelled. In the UK, ingenta is another consolidator, providing access through its ingentaJournals service to a growing number of publishers' journals.

An initial hope of many librarians was that a 'one-stop shop' would be established, allowing access to all electronic journals through one gateway. Given the proliferation of sources of such journals, this is perhaps now a hope unlikely to be completely realized, but perhaps one that is less important, provided that access through whichever source is made as straightforward and transparent as possible.

Electronic journal consortia

So far, we have discussed the acquisition of electronic journals by individual libraries. Consortia have a large and growing rôle here, as well as in the purchase of print journals – in many countries, consortia for electronic information acquisition have preceded and are much more important than print consortia. Indeed, a problem for many libraries is that they may belong to several different consortia, local, regional or national, usually pursuing slightly different aims, but with a real danger of confusion and overlap. Consortium administration can consume a significant proportion of the time available to some senior library staff, certainly including the serials librarian.

Consortia can and do negotiate with the different players mentioned above. In addition, in the UK, the government University Funding Councils have played an important part in encouraging the provision and take-up of electronic journals in the higher education sector, by acting as a sort of 'compulsory' consortium. The Funding Councils set up the Pilot Site Licence Initiative (PSLI) in 1996 with Academic Press, Blackwell, Blackwell Science, and Institute of Physics Publishing, to, among other things, provide electronic access to these publishers' journals (Bekhradnia, 1995). The funds for this were top-sliced from the UK university budget, and individual universities did not have to pay. This three-year 'national site licence' ran from 1996 to 1998 (to end-1999 for Academic Press), and was certainly very successful as a consciousness-raising exercise. Many academics, and indeed librarians, who had not previously paid much attention to electronic journals – very few were in fact available at that time – became aware of, and began to use, this new method of information provision.

PSLI has now been succeeded by the National Electronic Site Licence Initiative (NESLI), promoted by the Joint Information Systems Committee (JISC) of the Higher Education Funding Councils, with Swets Subscription Service and Manchester Computing together acting as managing agent (Friend, 1999; Woodward, 1999). NESLI is designed to be, or become, self-financing, and is negotiating electronic access deals with individual journal publishers, which are then put out to university libraries for acceptance or rejection on a library-by-library basis. The licence on which the agreements are based is modelled on the (UK) Publishers Association/JISC licence mentioned in Chapter 2 (PA/JISC, 1999). This approach has had some success, although it is too early to say what the long-term future of NESLI is likely to be.

Although the emphasis so far has been on the UK, consortia for negotiating access to electronic journals operate in many other countries. In Europe, examples exist in countries such as Finland, Germany, Greece (Kohl and Dervos, 1999) and Spain (Anglada, 1999), while Canada is developing its own National

Site Licensing Project, but the original home of such consortia is the USA, with many examples such as OhioLINK (Sanville and Winters, 1998; Sanville, 1999) and NELINET. The International Coalition of Library Consortia (ICOLC) was set up as an informal grouping in the USA in 1997, and has been a powerful force in disseminating information and best practice among consortia. Its first European meeting was held in December 1999, and it has published guidelines on setting out requests for proposals to publishers (ICOLC, 1999) and on statistical measurement of electronic journal usage (ICOLC, 1998).

Other sources of supply

Returning now to the subject of serials in general, it can sometimes be appropriate to use specialist suppliers, rather than serials agents, for print titles. Government publications, for example, can usually be acquired direct from the issuing body, normally The Stationery Office in the UK, or the US Government Printing Office in the USA. There are also firms specializing in this area that can obtain serials from the growing number of government departments which produce their own publications, and from various European and international bodies, such as the EU, OECD, the United Nations and its agencies, etc.

Libraries sometimes use different suppliers for serials from particular parts of the world, such as Russia and Eastern Europe, where supply has traditionally been problematic (Hogg, 1999). These suppliers can often provide a more intensive service with a greater knowledge of local conditions, though sometimes at slightly greater cost. However, most of the large international agents do now have offices in such 'difficult' areas, and their services can also be tested and utilized.

Finally, it is still sometimes sensible to place orders with individual publishers or societies. Occasionally, they refuse to deal via agents, and so direct orders are the only acquisition route. Many societies provide 'membership' or 'package' deals, although these are often now available through agents. In general, while it is very unlikely that any library will obtain every one of its journal titles through its chosen subscription agents, pressure on staff time will usually indicate that acquisition via an agent is the most cost-effective option.

Gifts/exchanges

Many libraries still receive a large number of serials via donation, or via exchanges. It should be remembered that even donations are by no means cost-free additions to library stock. Missing issues will still have to be claimed (and gifted titles are particularly prone to suffer missing issues), the journal may have to be catalogued, the space occupied on the shelf has a cost, etc. So decisions on whether to accept the title should follow the same collection management criteria discussed in Chapter 3, taking into account of course that the subscription price is zero.

Gifted titles come from an assortment of different sources, and may include annual reports and other literature from companies and institutions, and titles from staff (but the library should not accept current issues bought at the 'individual' rate, where the publisher stipulates that these should not be passed on to a library), students and local residents. It is often appropriate to acknowledge the commencement of receipt of a gifted title, at least from an individual as opposed to an institution, but it is rarely necessary to acknowledge each issue.

A particular type of 'gifted journal' is the electronic journal freely available on the Internet. These do not require 'claiming' in the normal sense, nor do they take up space on the shelves, but they will need cataloguing and/or listing in the library's web pages – see Chapter 6 – and there should be a system for regularly checking the journals' URL. They should therefore only be added, like other titles, if their quality and subject matter is appropriate.

Exchange titles may be less common than in the past, but are still an important method of serials acquisition in some libraries. For those libraries with interests in the old Soviet Union and Eastern Europe, they were often the only method of acquiring many journals. That is less true at present, but exchanges are still important in that area (Lorkovic and Johnson, 1997). Exchanges can be very intricate and therefore time-consuming to administer, particularly if actual purchases are made to send to the exchangee library, and a balance has to be maintained. This type of exchange should probably be abandoned if possible, except by specialist institutions, unless it really is the only way to obtain some material.

Another type of exchange involves publications produced by a university department that are then available for exchange for perhaps similar serials from other universities or societies. These exchanges may have no direct monetary cost, at least to the library, but are still subject to the other costs outlined above. Nevertheless, this may still be a useful way to collect serials that might be very difficult to find through conventional channels.

Conclusion

This chapter has covered a wide range of methods of acquisition of serials, both print and electronic. Although only providing a bare outline in many respects, it does indicate the many aspects of 'acquisition' that must currently be considered by all those working in this area, while emphasizing that further changes will inevitably take place over the next few years.

References

American Chemical Society (1999) *Subscription information for ACS publications*, available at:
http://pubs.acs.org/journals/subscribe_info.html

Amiran, E and Unsworth, J (1991) Postmodern culture: publishing in the electronic medium, *Public-Access Computer Systems Review*, 2 (1), 67–76, available at:
http://info.lib.uh.edu/pr/v2/n1/amiran.2n1

Anglada, L M (1999) Working together, learning together: the Consortium of Academic Libraries of Catalonia, *Information Technology and Libraries*, 18 (3), 139–44, available at:
http://www.lita.org/ital/1803_anglada.html

Association of Subscription Agents
http://www.subscription-agents.org/

Association of Subscription Agents (1999) *Guidelines*, ASA, available at:
http://www.subscription-agents.org/guidelines.html

Ball, D and Wright, S (1997) Managing the market place: the consortium approach, *Serials*, 10 (3), 329–36.

Bekhradnia, B (1995) Pilot national site licence initiative for academic journals, *Serials*, 8 (3), 247–50.

Bell & Howell Information and Learning
http://www.umi.com/

Benjamin, M (1999) International Committee on EDI for Serials (ICEDIS), *Learned Publishing*, 12 (3), 225–8.

Blackwell's Electronic Journal Navigator (EJN)
http://navigator.blackwell.co.uk/

British Library. *International Standard Serials Number*
http://www.bl.uk/information/issn.html

Brown, R (1999) What happens next? E-journals in the corporate information service, *Serials*, 12 (2), 149–52.

Bryn Mawr Classical Review
http://ccat.sas.upenn.edu/bmcr/

Canadian National Site Licensing Project
http://aix1.uottawa.ca/library/carl

Consortium of Academic Libraries in Manchester (CALIM)
http://rylibweb.man.ac.uk/calim/index.html

Council of the European Communities (1992) *Council Directive 92/50/EEC of 18 June 1992 relating to the coordination of procedures for the award of public service contracts.*

Davies, J (1999) Academic choices, *The Bookseller*, (26 November), 22–4.

EBSCO Online
http://www.ebsco.com/ess/services/online.stm

Electronic Information Distributors Association (EIDA)
   http://www.eida.ocd.fr/

Friend, F J (1999) New wine in a new bottle: purchasing by library consortia in the United Kingdom, *Information Technology and Libraries*, **18** (3), 145–8.

Hogg, R (1999) BLDSC acquisitions from eastern Europe, *Serials Librarian*, **35** (4), 71–93.

Information Quest
   http://www.informationquest.com/products.html

IngentaJournals
   http://www.ingenta.com/home/ingentaJournalsInfo.htm

International Coalition of Library Consortia (ICOLC)
   http://www.library.yale.edu/consortia/

International Coalition of Library Consortia (ICOLC) (1998) *Guidelines for statistical measures of usage of web-based indexed, abstracted and full-text resources*, available at: http://www.library.yale.edu/consortia/webstats.html

International Coalition of Library Consortia (ICOLC) (1999) *Guidelines for technical issues in request for proposal (RFP) requirements and contract negotiations*, available at:
   http://www.library.yale.edu/consortia/techreq.html

International Committee for EDI for Serials (ICEDIS)
   http://www.icedis.org/

ISSN International Centre
   http://www.issn.org/

ISSN Online
   http://www.issn.org/ISSNONLINE.html

Joint Funding Councils' Libraries Review Group (1993) *Report* [The Follett Report], Higher Education Funding Council for England, available at:
   http://www.ukoln.ac.uk/services/papers/follett/report/

Joint Funding Councils' Libraries Review Group (1995) *Report of the Group on a National Regional Strategy for Library Provision for Researchers* [The Anderson Report], Higher Education Funding Council for England, available at:
   http://www.ukoln.ac.uk/services/elib/papers/other/anderson/

Kohl, D and Dervos, C (1999) Getting acquainted: HEAL-Link, the Greek national academic library consortium, *Library Consortium Management*, **1** (3/4).

Lorkovic, T and Johnson, E A (1997) Serial and book exchanges with the former Soviet Union, *Serials Librarian*, **31** (4), 59–87.

Lyttle, T and Shorley, D (1994) Periodicals tendering for the libraries of the Queen's University of Belfast and the University of Ulster: a joint initiative, *Serials*, **7** (3), 221–6.

Merging subscription agents [editorial] (1999), *Learned Publishing*, **12** (3), 224.

National Electronic Site Licence Initiative (NESLI)
    http://www.nesli.ac.uk/
National Serials Data Program
    http://lcweb.loc.gov/issn/
NELINET
    http://www.nelinet.net/
OCLC. *Electronic Collections Online (ECO)*
    http://www.oclc.org/oclc/eco/main.htm
O'Donnell, J J (1996) Five years of Bryn Mawr Classical Review, *Serials Librarian*, **28**
    (3/4), 223–8.
OhioLINK
    http://www.ohiolink.edu/
Ovid Technologies
    http://www.ovid.com/
Postmodern Culture
    http://jefferson.village.virginia.edu/pmc/contents.all.html
Prior, A (1999) Electronic journals pricing – still in the melting pot? *Serials*, **12** (2),
    133–7.
Psycoloquy
    http://www.cogsci.soton.ac.uk/psycoloquy/
Publishers Association and Joint Information Systems Committee (1999) *Model
    licence between UK universities and publishers*, available at:
    http://www.ukoln.ac.uk/services/elib/papers/pa/ or
    http://www.library.yale.edu/~llicense/Pajisc21.html
Pye, J and Ball, D (1999) *Library purchasing consortia in the UK: activity, benefits and
    good practice: final report of BLRIC Research Project RIC/G/403*, Library and
    Information Commission.
Sanville, T J (1999) Use levels and new models for consortial purchasing of electronic
    journals, *Library Consortia Management*, **1** (3/4), 47–58.
Sanville, T J and Winters, B A (1998) A method out of the madness: OhioLINK's
    collaborative response to the serials crisis, *Serials Librarian*, **34** (1–2), 125–39.
Science
    http://www.sciencemag.org/
Scottish Confederation of University and Research Libraries (SCURL)
    http://bubl.ac.uk/org/scurl/
Serials Industry Systems Advisory Committee (SISAC)
    http://www.bisg.org/sisac.html
Snowley, I (1995) Tendering for periodicals supply: how librarians can manage the
    process, *Serials*, **8** (3), 227–30.
Southern Universities Purchasing Consortium (SUPC)
    http://www.exeter.ac.uk/SUPC/welcome.html

Spinella, M P (1999) Developing viable electronic journals, *Serials*, **12** (2), 111–17, available at:
http://www.uksg.org/serials/12/2/spinella.htm

The Stationery Office
http://www.tso-online.co.uk/

Summers, L (1995) ICEDIS: the International Committee for Electronic Data Interchange in Serials, *Serials*, **8** (3), 261–3.

SwetsNet
http://www.swetsnet.nl/

Taylor-Roe, J (1997) Consortia: what makes a negotiating unit? *Serials*, **10** (3), 307–12.

United States Government Printing Office
http://www.access.gpo.gov/

Woodward, H (1999) NESLI – the National Electronic Site Licence Initiative . . . creating a bit of a disturbance, *Serials*, **12** (1), 17–20.

6

Processing

Matthew Searle

Introduction

This chapter is concerned with the nuts and bolts of serials management within the library: keeping a catalogue record of titles to which the library provides access and recording the receipt of individual parts. It is oriented towards the use of an integrated automated library housekeeping system as typically installed in academic institutions.

Record keeping

The library's first duty on receiving the latest issue of a periodical is to make it available to its users as quickly as possible. It also needs to keep a record of what it has received. There are three reasons for this:

- to satisfy enquiries from users
- to maintain an audit trail, demonstrating that the library has received what it paid for
- to enable any omissions to be made good.

A library which receives its serials from a consolidation service or an outsourced service provider will equally need to ensure that it has access to the accompanying records. This might be, for example, by access to the supplier's database or by downloading data to the library's own management system. If a central library acts as a receiving station for a multi-site system, the receipt records need to be available to the branches.

In principle, the same type of records should be available for non-print journals. Delivery of an electronic journal from publisher to website ought to be both prompt and assured (even when this is not the case, there may be little that the library can do to encourage timely mounting of content), but ensuring that a library's access rights to data are maintained can be a problem. In addition to subscription payment and any technical arrangements for access, an electronic journal may require a signed agreement with the publisher and a serial delivered in CD-ROM format may involve the library in a networking licence, any of which may be renewable. As loss of service means loss of access to a run of issues, users are more likely to bring problems to the library's attention at an early stage, but librarians in general ought to be more proactive than reactive to such a situation.

A record of agreements with expiration dates and details of any special terms needs to be maintained and acted on when necessary. As regards the possibility of changing URLs or other possible technical barriers to access, suppliers of paid-for electronic journals should be taking responsibility for the maintenance of links. However, if the library has committed resources to the inclusion in its catalogue of free-access electronic journals it has in effect taken upon itself the responsibility for maintaining links on behalf of its users. Although link checking services are available, these are not likely to be able to explore the depth of service offered (some sites may offer abstract-only as an alternative to full-text level access depending on the library's customer status). This potential burden should be taken into account if considering offering such a service.

Manual systems

Manual record-keeping systems still have a place, particularly in the smaller operation, although it is increasingly difficult to find specialized stationery for the purpose. To avoid maintaining multiple files, it may be helpful to keep payment and issue receipt data in the same file, with the proviso that if sophisticated financial statistics are required, additional paperwork may be involved, or discussion with a serials vendor may produce data from their files which the library can utilize. Similarly, a vendor's consolidation service may be able to provide specialized labelling or other services if required. It is important to be consistent about whatever scheme of filing records is adopted so that new staff can easily learn the procedures.

Automated systems

The trend in recent years has been for libraries to record their serials receipts by using an automated system. The most recent UK survey (Walsh, 1994, 173–7) suggests a rapid and continuing uptake of serials modules, with government and research libraries leading the way. Most systems were bought in, with 15% of libraries scattered across all sectors using a system provided by their serials supplier, and around 44% using a commercial systems supplier, but at the time of the survey a perhaps surprising number of libraries with a serials module available to them as part of a general library management system had not acti-vated it. There are probably around 30 currently distributed library manage-ment systems, most with serials functionality, available in the UK. As companies, their contact details, and their products, all tend to change with some frequency, no attempt has been made to list or analyse them individually here. Updated details are often given in the Library Information Technology Centre's journal *Vine*; recent examples include Yeates (1998) and Yeates (1999).

The use of serials suppliers' systems is essentially confined to smaller library units. Where a library has limited staff resources which it will wish to devote to reader service functions, there is an advantage in buying what amounts to an all-in package of supply and system support from a single known source. The implication is that the library will have a single supplier relationship and also that – depending on exactly what package is on offer – integration of serials data with other library functions may not be important.

Any library considering adopting an automated serials system should be cer-tain that the reasons for replacing manual records have been fully thought through, since some of the features of automated systems traditionally quoted as benefits are not unambiguously so. The following are some of the points which need to be considered in relation to operating with such systems.

Visibility of data

Information about receipt (or non-receipt) and other processing of serial parts (eg circulation of current parts and binding) can be available to all the library's users and staff system-wide and for as long a period as the library system is run-ning, not merely for just as long as a member of serials staff is available to answer an enquiry. This is one of the main advantages of an automated system, particularly in a large and dispersed organization. A standalone system, or any method which does not deliver networked benefits, thus loses a key user advan-tage. Making data available so widely carries the implication that it must be not only accurate, but in a form that is intelligible to all users. Serials records should not be seen as administrative tools only: they are part of the package of infor-mation that the library delivers to its users. This may have implications for the skilling of serials staff.

Integration of data

Automated serials systems need to be viewed as integral to the library's total systems package. There are two viewpoints to consider:

1   For the library user, there should be a seamless interface which might perhaps carry through from initial search at article level in bibliographic databases to automatic look-up of the library catalogue, an option to select electronic access, and a check down to issue level of the library's paper holdings. Other scenarios can be envisaged, but the key point is that boundaries between library databases should be transparent to the user.

2   For library staff, integration should mean more focused record keeping. For example, a change of title may require amendments to catalogue, check-in and subscription data: ideally this should require as few actual alterations as possible, since relevant data fields will update interactively across the library management system. This has implications for staff organization and skills: at the least it may require the sort of close cross-departmental cooperation described by Goldberg and Neagle (1996) at Louisville University; going further, it may be an inefficient use of staff resource to think of some tasks relating to serials records to be 'serials administration' and others to be 'cataloguing' if this means splitting a job which could be done by one person.

Management information

The ideal to be aimed at is for the serials database to provide all such statistics, listings and other management information which the library requires without the necessity of maintaining records elsewhere. In general, library management systems seem not yet to perform especially well in this area, partly because database interrogation software is often too complex for anyone but a systems specialist to handle. Whether or not they are working through such an intermediary, serials librarians do need to have a good understanding of their database structure and of the purpose of any management enquiry in order to be able to ask the right questions.

It is especially useful to have live financial data available within an integrated system, since this will be the basis of much decision-making and thus a major component of management information. The extent to which this can be achieved depends on the degree to which the library can, or is obliged to, make use of any accounting package run by its parent organization. Procedures should retain as much relevant information as possible within the library's control, while eliminating as much duplication of effort in recording it as possible.

Speed and ease of processing

There are some elements of serials processing which can fairly be claimed to be faster with an automated than with a manual system. The mechanics of recording are probably faster, not least because pre-sorting into alphabetical (or other) order should be unnecessary. It is possible to consider checking in serials by scanning barcodes printed on the covers, but this depends on systems compatibility and a high proportion of titles received carrying barcodes in a uniform format (which will normally mean the SISAC barcode symbol), and is not widely adopted (Walsh, 1994, 175); it is perhaps worth consideration only if a very large throughput has to be maintained. Nevertheless, calling up records by means other than title search (even simply by manually keyed ISSN) can facilitate check-in, being especially useful where staff have to handle material in unfamiliar scripts or with complex title structures. Processing the annual renewal invoice in electronic format is a considerable time-saver, but the librarian needs to take into account the amount of control which is available (and required) over the loading process.

Against ease of processing at point of handling needs to be set the additional burden of record maintenance which does not arise with a manual system: the construction and maintenance of prediction patterns. The impact of this will vary from system to system, and, particularly during any setting-up stage, it is worth investigating whether any kind of collaboration with other libraries might be helpful. Libraries should consider the implications of this aspect of processing on staff skills: whilst it could be argued that the mechanics of automated check-in require less skill, this is really true only if the underlying records are optimally maintained, a task which calls for some judgment.

Claiming

Traditionally the ability to maintain a timely and comprehensive claiming routine for missing parts is said to be one of the benefits of an automated serials system. This is certainly true in general terms, particularly for larger collections, but oversimplifies the situation. If a periodical is ordinarily published in a straightforward sequence without deviation and at highly regular intervals, it is easy for any system to detect variations from the norm. The nearer publication approaches to irregularity, the more difficult it becomes for a system to detect deviation. Suppliers have been known to say that 65% of all claims received by them are too early; it would be interesting to know what proportion are automatically generated. In any case, too many false claims do no good for relationships in the serial supply chain. If the library is to avoid flooding its suppliers with unnecessary claims, a good deal of manual intervention is likely to be called for, either in the editing of parameters and patterns or in the weeding of claims during the generation process (and if the library is to avoid flooding itself with paper, there is much to be said for editing and, ideally, transmitting claims online).

Access to publisher information on publication dates and claim limits will assist the library, and this can often be obtained from suppliers' databases. Automated serials systems marketed by serial subscription agencies are perhaps better attuned to handling eccentricities of publication than those from general systems suppliers; this is, after all, a core aspect of the agent's business. It is desirable for there to be system provision to annotate records with vendor reports. More work is needed by system developers on ways in which supplier information and reports can be handled by electronic data interchange (EDI). Development thought also needs to be given to intelligent systems which learn from previous receipt patterns.

Incidentally, it follows from this that libraries should be very wary of taking system-generated statistics of response to claims as a valid measure of serials vendor performance: guidance on this has been produced by the Association for Library Collections & Technical Services (1997).

Looking for a new system
Specification

Bearing in mind some of the potential benefits and disadvantages of working with an automated serials system, what should the library be looking for in a new or (perhaps more likely today) replacement or upgraded system? Of course, the serials element will typically form just one module of a total library systems package and must be considered in that context: Murray (1997) reviews some recent UK procurements in this way. It is important when investigating systems to remember that serials management is not likely to be confined within the serials module: subscriptions will very probably be managed within the acquisitions function, and cataloguing within its own module. In the procurement process, an outcome-based specification should be aimed at; that is to say, the library should set out the ends the system should meet, not the way in which it gets there. Matters to take into account when considering a system include:

- Ease of day-to-day operation – what keystrokes or other actions are required to carry out routine tasks? What essential processing information is available at point of check-in?
- Will the system handle all tasks that the library needs, eg circulation of current issues or production of labels?
- Ease of maintenance – how easily and comprehensively can administrative functions be carried out?

- Migration of records – how will records be migrated from any earlier system? How will this retrospective data display on the OPAC?
- Relationship with catalogue – how well does serials information, particularly local data, display on the OPAC? What functions carried out by library staff impact on the public display?
- Claiming – what algorithms trigger claims, and what is the effect of manual intervention in the process?
- Invoicing – how does the acquisitions/fiscal control module handle indefinitely open orders (characteristic of serials), together with variations such as additional payments and one-off orders for replacement issues?
- Binding – how does the system track parts through the binding process? Does it automatically consolidate records for individual issues into records for bound volumes?
- Compatibility with external software, eg vendor EDI (including electronic invoicing), institutional accounting system, local area network, bibliographic databases (intranet and Internet), electronic journals.
- Conformity to appropriate international standards, eg ANSI, MARC, Z39.50.
- Availability and ease of use of management information.

In evaluating a system, the library will need to weight functionality against its individual needs, for example the ability to handle complex publication patterns may be especially important to a library handling a large amount of legal material, which frequently presents complex combinations of incrementing and updating services.

When the system is in place, the library should be organized to formulate and transmit proposals for enhancement through user groups or whatever mechanisms are available to it.

Planning and implementation

Erler-Stelz (1995) and Searle (1999) give portraits of serial system implementation in contrasting types of library. In any automation exercise there are a couple of basic questions which the library should ask of itself:

- Are library processes optimally tailored to the system's functionality? If not, which should change?
- Are staff appropriately skilled and deployed for the work? If not, what training or restructuring is required?

More practical matters to be taken into account in implementing a new system will include:

- any requirement for pre-implementation retrospective cataloguing
- prior annotation or other preparation of manual records for ease of transfer
- prior decision on handling of non-standard categories of material (eg serial parts catalogued as monographs in series)
- decision on timetabling of transfer of manual records.

Choosing whether to make the changeover as a 'big bang' or a more gradual approach will depend largely on what extra staff resource will be available to undertake the project (typically, nil); likewise, the choice of working through records in sequence, converting them as and when issues are received, or concentrating on records which can most quickly be converted, will depend on which method will most efficiently get the work done within the particular library context. Obviously, the serials manager must maintain a clear picture of the state of transfer throughout the project; equally, reader services staff should be made aware of the programme of implementation so that they can know which records should be used for answering reader enquiries.

If there is any choice over the time of year for implementing a new system, aiming to go live with the start of a new year (and new volumes of periodicals) is quite a good choice; in any case it makes sense with a new implementation to record issues retrospectively back to some such clearly defined starting date. Implementation whilst renewal invoices are being processed in the autumn or when end-of-financial-year statistics are being collated is definitely not to be recommended.

A change of system should be viewed as an opportunity to purge the database. There would, for example, be little point in setting up an automated record for the check-in of a donated title whose manual record suggested its possible demise.

Consideration must be given to how many and what level of staff should attend the systems supplier's training session and who will receive 'trickle-down' training. Before effective training can be delivered to more junior staff, some basic decisions on library-specific practices will have to be made. It is good practice to document these at once, even though more experience is likely to lead to revisions. If the number of staff involved in implementation is of any size, regular debriefing meetings will be valuable in developing procedures; and if contact has been made with another library prepared to pass on advice, that too will be appreciated when some practical experience of the system has been gained.

Cataloguing

With the possible exception of libraries operating within closed communities (as with corporate information services), it is highly desirable to adhere exactly to standard cataloguing conventions and data exchange protocols – which in practice usually means the use of AACR2 and MARC in catalogue records and Z39.50 compliant systems. This is not so much (as it is with monographs) because of the advantages of sharing records at the initial cataloguing stage, since for most libraries the addition of a completely new serial title to the catalogue is, comparatively speaking, a rare event, unless a retrospective cataloguing programme is in operation. The reasons are primarily concerned with compatibility in the following four areas:

1   With the underlying structure of library housekeeping systems. The major commercially available library systems utilize a MARC structure of records; this makes for commonality of understanding between systems supplier and client and has commercial advantage for a developer selling into global markets.
2   With union lists. The idea of the union list, virtually abandoned as unmanageable in the print age, has been revived in electronic forms, exemplified by COPAC and OCLC WorldCat (Enriching WorldCat, 1998), or for example the SALSER database of Scottish academic libraries' serials records, which depend on the sharing of library records in common formats, and there is a reasonable expectation on the part of readers and public funding bodies that libraries will exchange information on their resources (particularly important in the case of serials given the relentless cycle of cancellations in recent years). The way in which interlibrary loans operations place increasing reliance on such sources is described by Myers (1996).
3   With bibliographic databases. If linking from a bibliographic database, or, indeed, from an electronic article, to serial title level in the library's own catalogue is required, account needs to be taken of the operative standards.
4   With personal bibliographic software. If library users or information professionals wish to use commercial personal bibliographic packages to download information from the catalogue, it needs to be structured in a way that can be handled by the software.

How far the library adheres strictly to cataloguing rules depends upon its commitment to compatibility. The variability over time of a serial as a bibliographic entity makes it difficult to catalogue in a way that retains current usefulness, and discussions on the future development of AACR (Hirams and Graham, 1998) suggest modifications to the rules to reflect more helpfully the dynamic nature of serials, for example citing the current publisher of the title, instead of or in addition to the publisher of the first issue.

Local catalogue data

Whereas a monograph typically has just two levels of record, bibliographic and copy, a serial in a library which checks in paper issues using an automated system typically has at least three levels, bibliographic, copy set (representing the location at which a run of the title is held) and item (representing the individual part). Moreover, the item level record may itself represent a separate bibliographic entity (as for a monograph in series or a special issue catalogued separately); ideally there should be reciprocal system links allowing the user to identify and locate an item either as a monograph or a serial part. Libraries which bind paper copies will want to record the removal of parts from the shelves for binding so that users and reader services staff can trace this information from the OPAC. Finally, the records for individual issues should be conflated to reflect the composition of bound volumes, thus introducing a fourth level of local record. All this will be particularly significant where a library circulates periodicals, since it will need to be able to utilize whichever level of local record it needs as a circulation record; the same principle will apply if a library operates a request system for fetching from closed stacks.

Do catalogue records for electronic serials need local data? If the library networks a resource delivered on a physical carrier (typically, a CD-ROM), it may with good reason wish to register receipt of current issues; the library may also need some form of local holdings data on which to hang its subscription record. This, however, is information primarily of administrative interest, and the library may wish to suppress it from public display if its system permits. Whether the library needs a holdings record for material which is remotely accessed and thus not actually held depends on overall decisions made about the cataloguing of electronic serials. Somewhere in the catalogue record the library should include the coverage dates available to its users by electronic means, since these will probably differ from the library's paper holdings.

Cataloguing remotely accessed electronic serials

This is an area of considerable current interest and concern, but also one in which the development of universally agreed standards lags behind the increasingly urgent requirement for libraries to undertake the task.

A quick solution very widely adopted is to create library web pages giving lists of electronically available resources and providing direct links to them; these might be databases on the institutional intranet or remotely accessed electronic journals, as described by Moothart (1996). This can provide good publicity for the existence of the resources included. Care should be taken to avoid arbitrary division of the resources by categories such as carrier or service provider: in general, library users have no desire or need to know about the mechanisms by which material is delivered to them. Alphabetical and subject arrangements are of much more use.

A variant of this is to use an aggregator's interface, assuming the library has enough electronic subscriptions in a single aggregator's basket to make this a sensible option. In this case, the library will probably wish to ensure that the front end is tailorable so that only the titles to which it offers full-text access are listed: users are apt to become frustrated at lists which appear to promise much but lead only to a refusal of access.

The great disadvantage of using a web serials listing as a sole access point is that it is incompatible with the concept of the hybrid library. Unless the library is so radical as to have abandoned everything but electronic resources, they are going to be in use alongside related conventionally printed and conventionally catalogued material: even if the library does not offer print and electronic journals in parallel, it is virtually certain that its older back runs will be available only in print (except where it has digitized older material and only the more modern is in hard copy). A hybrid library needs a single finding aid: users interested in a particular serial should be able to check in one place whether their institution provides access to it and to choose whether to consult it within the library or remotely; if the latter choice is available, the finding aid should also contain a delivery mechanism. The web is certainly the right site for constructing a catalogue of electronic serials, but it should be as part of a web-based OPAC and not as a separate list. In the longer view, the idea of an OPAC as a distinctively separate entity is obsolescent: a single institutional website should deliver access to the institution's resources and only if the searcher chooses should a search focus on one particular delivery medium.

Current conventions treat the electronic version of a printed serial as a separate bibliographic entity, thus requiring a separate catalogue entry from that for the paper copy. There are cases where this is difficult to argue with: if an electronic version is the only one available (or the only one to which the library has access), where the content of the electronic version differs from print, or where the title of the electronic version is distinctive. But in the case of parallel print and electronic publishing, the catalogue user really needs to see at a glance which versions are available. Discussion on the future development of AACR (Howarth, 1998) suggests the adoption of three levels of record (content, format and item) which would meet the situation. Until new conventions are established, libraries must choose how best to display the information: for example, by adding notes, URLs and pseudo-holdings data to records for paper copies, or by creating dynamic links between records representing different access modes. For those using MARC records, field 856 is available for linking entries.

It will also be necessary to provide dynamic links to the electronic title. Consideration needs to be given to where the links are pointing: to the library's own web page, to an aggregator's site, to the publisher's home page, to the journal home page? The choice depends on the way in which the library's clientele customarily use journals. If they are accustomed to approach the OPAC already armed with references and seeking specific issues, they will probably appreciate being linked as closely as technical and contractual restraints permit to the list of issues available. If mirror sites or alternative aggregators' gateways are available, the library needs to choose its optimal access route. It must be remembered that links can change, and, if they are embedded in other records, or if they are changed for contractual reasons, it may not be easy to use link checking software to assist: there is the likelihood of a continuing record maintenance liability. A promising technical solution is the use of metadata to provide links (and also, potentially, the basis of catalogue records); but this too waits on establishment and widespread adoption of internationally agreed standards, such as Dublin Core (Dempsey and Heery, 1998; Weibel, 1999). Another consideration for the library in setting up access routes to electronic serials is the desire to monitor usage. This is a poorly developed area at present, with no clearly established principles as to what, for example, constitutes 'use' of an electronic title; however, given that there is potentially valuable information available, the library will want to arrange matters so that usage statistics will be collected for all titles and in a consistent manner.

Classification

Whether and how a library chooses to classify its serials is a matter of individual preference and dependent on its general policy towards classification and on whether it chooses to shelve its hard copy serials in any form of classified sequence. This is not an area which receives, or perhaps deserves, much attention: the customary and most satisfactory approach to a serial collection is to the content via bibliographical indexing services rather than to titles by subject, although browsing of print issues of related titles is still important for many academics. Academic libraries are likely to have financial structures which require them to account for their subscriptions by subject, but this information is more likely to be obtained via the library system's accounting function than from catalogue data.

The OPAC display

Assuming the OPAC front end display is, at least to some extent, within the library's control, decisions are needed about how, and how much, serials data is to be displayed. Use specifically of serials information on OPACs is an area which needs research. There is usually a user demand for the ability to pre-restrict the search to serials only. Provision of keyword search is particularly important given that the *exact* form of a serial title is not by any means always known to the searcher. One of the bugbears of serials, title changes, can be mitigated in a web-based catalogue by the use of dynamic links. It is desirable for the display to be configurable differently for different types of material, eg the date of publication, which is important for monographs, can be actually misleading for a serial where the library does not hold a complete run; emphasis should always be given to the library's actual holdings.

Some library systems will construct a holdings display from check-in data. This is superficially attractive, but of questionable value for two reasons. First, the library's holdings prior to its use of an automated system need to be consolidated into such a statement for it to be useful; and, secondly, unless receipt of the title has proceeded with remarkable smoothness, an over-complex statement is likely to result. Some form of manual override is desirable. Users searching the OPAC should be able to tell at a glance whether the library holds it and where. It is also useful if the OPAC can easily answer the very common question, 'Have you received the latest issue yet?'; this is of more practical importance than 'What is the next issue expected?', which some systems emphasize. Supplementary information such as receipt data for earlier issues and binding records is best located in a second level display.

Conclusion

The key feature of library processing of serials using the current generation of housekeeping systems is integration: between electronic and paper serials; between cataloguing and administrative data; and between administrative and public data. The aim is to keep a core of information with different views depending on whether access or management information is required. Above all, systems should facilitate and not obstruct user access to material.

References

Association for Library Collections & Technical Services, Serials Section, Acquisitions Committee (1997) *Guide to performance evaluation of serials vendors*, American Library Association.

COPAC
>http://www.copac.ac.uk/

Dempsey, L and Heery, R (1998) Metadata: a current view of practice and issues, *Journal of Documentation*, **54** (2), 145–72.

Enriching WorldCat (1998), *OCLC Newsletter*, **233**, 34–42, available at:
>http://www.oclc.org/oclc/new/n233/index.htm

Erler-Stelz, T (1995) Practical experience with the serials control package 'SAILS', *Serials Librarian*, **26** (2), 75–85.

Goldberg, T and Neagle, E (1996) Serials information in the OPAC: a model for shared responsibility, *Serials Review*, **22** (4), 55–63.

Hawkins, L (1998) Serials published on the World Wide Web: cataloging problems and decisions, *Serials Librarian*, **33** (1/2), 123–45.

Hirams, J and Graham, C (1998) Issues related to seriality. In Weihs, J (ed) *The principles and future of AACR*, Library Association Publishing.

Howarth, L C (1998) Content versus carrier. In Weihs, J (ed) *The principles and future of AACR*, Library Association Publishing.

MacAdam, C (ed) (1996) Selecting the serials module of an integrated library system, *Serials Review*, **22** (2), 79–91.

Moothart, T (1996) Providing access to e-journals through library home pages, *Serials Review*, **22** (2), 71–7.

Murray, I R (1997) Assessing the effect of new generation library management systems, *Program*, **31** (4), 313–27.

Myers, M (1996) Union listing on OCLC past, present and future, *Serials Review*, **22** (2), 45–51.

SALSER
>http://edina.ed.ac.uk/salser/

Searle, M (1999) Serials housekeeping in a federal setting, *Serials*, **12** (1), 47–9.

Walsh, P (1994) UKSG serials automation survey 1994, *Serials*, **7** (2) , 173–7.

Weibel, S (1999) The state of the Dublin Core metadata initiative April 1999, *D-Lib Magazine*, **5** (4), available at:
>http://www.dlib.org/dlib/april99/04weibel.html

Yeates, R (1998) Year 2000 compliant systems in the library sector, *Vine*, **108**, 74–8.

Yeates, R (1999) Library management systems: for special libraries, *Vine*, **110**, 48–54, available at:
>http://agent.sbu.ac.uk/publications/vine/110/special.html

7

Stock management

Liz Stevenson

Introduction

As libraries move towards the virtual future, the practice of stock management could be seen as approaching redundancy as increasing provision of electronic access reduces the growth of physical collections. For the foreseeable future however, most libraries' collections will be a mix of print and electronic, with the care and management of physical collections remaining important and resource-intensive issues.

Stock management is a key part of the process of serials control and is most effective if it is part of an overall collection management policy developed in consultation with users, subject specialists and library staff, reflecting the needs and aims of the library service. Acquisitions staff are well placed to have a broad perspective on the process (Law, 1999, 17). There should be flexibility and awareness of the changing needs of library users, taking full account of all the developments in teaching and research and in information provision (Hitchingham, 1996, 41).

Evaluation of existing collections must form a starting point for any policy. Diminishing budgets, journal inflation, the high cost of provision of electronic data and the associated infrastructure all form a constant backdrop to decision making. Important issues to consider are the shifting balance between expenditure on print and electronic resources, between expenditure on monograph and journal provision, and between locally held collections and a high quality document delivery service.

Physical collections are predominantly print, supplemented over the last 30 years by microform and more recently by electronic media, including CD-ROM, electronic journals and growing collections of digitized materials. Early perceptions were that the growth of the electronic journal would threaten print collections, but until longer-term solutions are found, at least to the archiving, access and ownership issues associated with electronic journals, print will remain central to most collections.

Academic and special libraries invest considerable funds in serials collections and whether retention is short or long term, the serials librarian should ensure that the collection is in good order.

The following sections will examine the areas of storage and shelving, withdrawal and disposal, routing and circulation, preservation, and archiving.

Storage and shelving

Current collections are usually held on open access, with latest issues placed on appropriate display shelving, making it easier for users to browse new stock. This can be done using sloping display shelves, which may also have space underneath for storage of precurrent issues. Alternatively, precurrent issues are shelved with backruns of the journal, stored upright in acid-free cardboard boxes, or stored flat on the shelf. Good storage should help protect stock. If appropriate boxes are not an option, then unbound material is best stored flat, to ensure even distribution of weight and reduce the risk of buckling. This is not a practical option for long backruns, which ideally should be bound, or stored in boxes. Annual statistics of serials accessions should help as a guide for estimating the growth of stock, to help plan additional space for stock expansion. Guidelines issued in the UK by SCONUL (Standing Conference of National and University Libraries, 1999) suggest a figure of an average of 18 bound periodical volumes per metre.

Compact rolling shelving is space saving and is commonly used to shelve extensive backruns of journals, usually for closed access collections. Appropriate trade catalogues give details of the different types of shelving available, including sizings and cost. It is worth consulting other libraries for advice or warnings about the suitability of particular types of shelving.

Newspapers present their own particular problems. Unless they are being retained as an archive, newspapers are ideally held for a limited period only. Microform, CD-ROM or online versions can provide manageable archive copy.

Arrangement of the collections

There are a number of options to consider when planning the arrangement of a journal collection. The following issues are regularly raised for discussion on e-mail listserv groups and there is no consensus as to the best practice:

- Is it better to arrange journals by subject or alphabetically by title?
- Should current issues be shelved with backruns?
- Should journals be interfiled with book collections or maintained as a separate collection?

- Should microform, or other media, be shelved alongside print?

Large academic libraries are more likely to be able to offer discrete areas for journals, with a current display area adjoining the collection of backruns, and staff on hand to deal with enquiries. Many libraries have arrived at current practice through expedience rather than through careful planning, and existing arrangements may not always reflect the best option for users or library staff. If current journals are shelved apart, they should ideally be shelved in the same order as backruns. A collection which is subject specific can justifiably be arranged by title, making it easier for users to find items without recourse to the library catalogue, and making reshelving a straightforward operation for library staff. A broader-based collection benefits from subject subdivision, based on the library's subject classification. The subject approach also ensures that title changes do not disrupt the run of the journal. In this case, it is important to have clearly labelled shelves, readily available serials listings or access to the library catalogue, enabling users to identify the shelf location. If the collection is arranged by title, there need to be appropriate markers on the shelves to indicate previous and continuing titles.

Microfilms are best stored individually in boxes either in customized cabinets, or on open shelves. The publishers will usually supply suitable storage boxes. Microfiche material should be stored in either customized cabinets or folders with individual pockets for each microfiche. This helps to keep the collection in order and reduces the risk of scratching or other damage. It can be awkward and impractical to store microform backruns with print copies of the same title, but appropriate signage should direct users to the corresponding print collection. If possible, microform readers and copiers should be close by.

Discards and withdrawals

Why should libraries withdraw or even discard material? This question may not arise until space for current collections is at a premium, or if space is needed for other purposes. However, it should form part of the process of stock management, following agreed guidelines within the library's collection management policy. Many users' needs may be met by retaining only five to ten years' worth of printed material, thereafter relying on other formats such as microform, CD-ROM, electronic journals or on document delivery. More is not necessarily better and the best practice should be to have systems in place to ensure retention of what is most relevant and cost-effective to meet the immediate and long term needs of users. Decisions should not be taken just on the grounds of expedience but rather as part of a stated process of examining the collection as whole. New directions in teaching or research will determine new acquisitions, and this process may also help to highlight outdated material that is no longer relevant to the collections. Surveys of use, and evaluation of titles by impact factor or half life, can inform such decisions, but there does need to be qualitative assessment as well as quantitative. It may prove worthwhile to discard print in favour of an electronic archive, such as JSTOR. The analogy with gardening is a good one – weeding out whatever is clogging up a collection and stifling its growth.

What can be discarded? Superseded reference material can usually be discarded as a matter of course, as can print copies of titles which are also held in other media eg newspapers or journals retained on microfilm or on CD-ROM. Stock that is not heavily used, but which still has a place in the collections, such as older runs of journals which are no longer current, may be relegated to a closed stack or to a remote store but still remain available on demand. If practicable, it is helpful to record usage, particularly of material in store, and to use this evidence to inform longer-term decisions on whether or not a title should be retained or discarded. Titles no longer relevant to users' needs, titles that are very rarely used, titles that are infrequently used but are available locally elsewhere, should be considered for withdrawal or even disposal, in consultation with users. All such changes to holdings or locations must be recorded in the library catalogue and any serials holdings lists.

Disposal

Stock disposal is a contentious issue which needs to be handled sensitively and decisions taken in consultation with users. This involves users in the process and invites their cooperation. If reasons for disposal are given, and other options are suggested, this can be presented as a positive process to help improve collections, and to make better use of diminishing resources.

Material can be offered to other libraries either by circulating lists to potential sites, or by e-mailing a listserv, offering the material free but asking the receiving library to pay postage and packing costs. It is important to recognize the costs of undertaking such an exercise – listing and advertising titles and corresponding with interested sites takes time. Some examples of current listservs are listed on the US *Back Issues & Exchange Services* website; a UK example in the medical area is the *lis-medjournal-duplicates* list, which processes 40 to 50 messages each month. A *Journals Exchange Scheme* has also recently been set up by BUBL, the Strathclyde University based electronic information service, supported by the UK Higher Education Funding Councils' Joint Information Systems Committee (JISC). Other disposal options are pulping, sale or offer to library users, or sale to the trade, to specialist back issue dealers. This last option may not be a great fund-raiser but it does ensure that material is handled quickly and effectively and should take up the minimum of staff time.

A library book sale, though, is an opportunity for users to buy unwanted stock, both books and journals, cheaply. If well managed, a sale can provide a valuable public relations exercise for the library. It is important to carefully screen material for sale and, if possible, to invite selected users to check the stock to ensure that what is withdrawn is unwanted. The staff time taken to organize these events can be considerable. A simple pricing process, rather than costing items individually, is advisable.

If space permits, it is best to organize withdrawn stock so as to minimize double-handling. On final withdrawal the library catalogue should be amended. Each part or volume should have all marks of ownership clearly labelled as 'Withdrawn' or 'Cancelled'.

Routing and circulation

The level of routing or internal circulation of current issues varies depending on the practice and culture of an institution. In special libraries material is more likely to be routed to users, forming part of a more extensive current awareness service. Libraries within large academic institutions often operate a restricted routing system as a current awareness service for a closed group, such as library staff. The need for this diminishes as automatic electronic notification of pub-lication and content increases, and with specialist alerting services such as BUBL, which maintains a constantly updated listing of contents and abstracts for journals relevant to the library and information profession (Dawson, 1999). Issues are often routed to special interest groups, with a membership listing attached. Within academic libraries the issue would normally be returned to serials administration once all members have seen it. A more controlled routing is where an issue is sent to each individual member, who then returns it to source before it is sent to the next member of the group. Such procedures may not be the case in special libraries, where key titles form part of a working col-lection within departments and the purchase of multiple copies of such titles is an option. Increasingly now, the alternative is to buy a network licence to access such titles electronically, thereby reducing processing costs while catering to demand.

Automated check-in systems will usually provide a routing option, which will print routing slips automatically and will enable members to check which titles they regularly see. It is worth reviewing this process on a regular basis, asking users to confirm that they still need (or have time to) read or scan new issues.

The circulation, or lending, of journals depends on the needs of the organization and its users. Many libraries do not lend journals, but may lend bound backruns for limited periods, with even more restricted loan periods for unbound material. Most users need to browse contents or to access only one or two articles from a volume. Borrowing an issue or volume for any length of time disadvantages other users. Adequate photocopying facilities and quick reshelving should mean that material is available as widely and as speedily as possible after use.

Preservation

Material which is to be retained for a length of time needs to be cared for, and either bound or stored appropriately. To bind or not to bind? If material is only retained for a limited period then it is unlikely to be necessary to bind, and storage in appropriate acid-free boxes will suffice, although this does increase the risk of theft. Binding preserves and brings together all issues in a volume, usually with an index, and helps to reduce the risk of theft or loss.

The type of binding chosen will depend on the likely level of use and on the reasons for retention. The format of the journal itself may not prove suitable for binding. If margins are too narrow then it is probably better to store the material in a cardboard casing, or box. A high specification binding should be used for material to be kept as an archive, and for material likely to be heavily used and photocopied. Traditional styles may not always sit well with repeated photocopying and a solution might be to adopt flatback binding (Woodward, 1999, 175). Alternative cheaper styles or casings are options for titles likely to be little used. Some larger libraries can still maintain in-house bindery departments, but most libraries will rely on the services of a commercial bindery. The library binder will retain records of the type and colour of binding chosen for each title, the spine lettering and any library-specific instructions such as whether security triggers or loan slips are to be included in the volume. This formula is commonly known as the rub.

Many library system suppliers now include binding control modules in their integrated systems, thus improving the storage of this information and reducing the need for duplication of record-keeping within a library. All binding instructions, rub details and dates of transactions can be recorded and make it possible to track progress of work more readily. Often such a system can generate reports of material ready for binding, thus saving staff time in checking records and shelves. The timing of journal binding can be awkward. It is inevitable that an issue or volume will be in demand as soon as it is withdrawn for binding! In a small collection it is possible to schedule binding batches at times when demand is low, but this is unlikely to be a realistic option in larger libraries where a rolling binding programme is in operation. Libraries should ensure as far as possible that the management of this process is not at the expense of users' needs. A speedy turnaround is essential and should be part of the library's contract or service level agreement with the binder.

Alternatives to binding

If costs limit binding, unbound parts should be stored in suitable boxes and should be bundled carefully using tape. Heavy use, poor handling and repeated photocopying all take their toll. Library staff training should include guidance on material handling. Repairs should be dealt with promptly and library staff should have training and guidelines on how and when to handle minor repairs such as paper tears or replacing single loose pages. It is worth taking advice on this from a binder or conservation expert to ensure that the correct materials are used.

Deliberate vandalism is a continuing problem in libraries, whether by marking the text, or removal of pages. If funds permit, the simplest solution is to replace missing or damaged pages, either by purchasing a replacement issue, or by obtaining photocopies of the missing pages, ensuring that the appropriate copyright permission has been sought and any fees paid. Theft of issues or volumes occurs, and a decision must then be taken on replacement, particularly if there is the risk of material going out of print.

These processes all involve costs, which will reduce funding available for other materials. The electronic journal offers an elegant solution to all these problems and, for the most part, does not require the user to visit the library in person.

Archiving

Any library collection, whether one year or 500 years old, can be seen as an archive. Archives of older material may be held off-site, or on closed access, and are unlikely to be in high demand. The archive could be part of a shared local repository, although there are costs and policy issues to consider. The issue of archiving is not a difficult one for print or microform subscriptions, as the physical object is owned by the library. Libraries buy the right to retain, shelve and display the journal, to advertise its availability via the library catalogue and to allow any library user to consult or photocopy material (M Smith, 1998, 136).

Archiving is not yet as straightforward with electronic collections. Typically, a library buys a networking licence giving accredited users the right to access the journal, whether the journal is available on a local network or via a publisher's server on the world wide web. Licence agreements restrict access and, within many institutions, online access may not be freely available to all users but only to those eligible to register under the agreement.

At present, electronic archives are limited and often only extend back to 1995 or so, but a growing number of publishers are working towards retrospective digitization of backfiles. Access to electronic archives may only be live while there is a current subscription although some publishers will offer a CD-ROM archive once a subscription is cancelled and the NESLI Model Licence includes provision for archive access. Projects are in place to take this forward and initiatives such as JSTOR, OCLC Electronic Collections Online and the eLib CEDARS project are all working towards a resolution of electronic journal archival issues.

Costs and copyright restrictions mean that libraries cannot tackle this individually, and at present, most publishers and aggregators, such as subscription agents, cannot truly undertake to guarantee long-term access. In the United Kingdom there is no legal deposit requirement for non-print publications. This is currently under review, and a voluntary pilot scheme is planned to establish how best to manage this process for electronic monographs and journals (G Smith, 1999, 125–9). The same issues of storage and licence apply, and will need careful control and monitoring. Provided they are properly managed, print and microfilm collections are available indefinitely, but there is no present guarantee of similar access to electronic journals. This situation must be resolved before there can be a wholesale abandonment of print in favour of electronic provision.

Conclusion

Librarians no longer think solely in terms of ownership of collections. Library managers will increasingly move service provision and budgets to improved document delivery to the end-user. The virtual library will provide a gateway, or portal, to what the user needs, and the librarian will not be primarily the owner and keeper of the material but the facilitator of its use. However, for the foreseeable future, the 'hybrid library' of combined print and electronic holdings and access is likely to be a more viable model, and stock management of both print and electronic materials will continue to be an important part of the portfolio of skills of the serials librarian.

References

Back Issues & Exchange Services
http://www.uvm.edu/~bmaclenn/backexch.html
BUBL Information Service

http://www.bubl.ac.uk/

BUBL Journals Exchange Scheme

http://www.bubl.ac.uk/org/dups

The CEDARS Project

http://www.leeds.ac.uk/cedars/

Dawson, A (1999) Inferring user behaviour from journal access figures, *Serials Librarian*, **35** (3), 31–41, available at:

http://www.bubl.ac.uk/journals/lis/oz/serlib/v35n0399/dawson.htm

Hitchingham, E (1996) Collection management in the light of electronic publishing, *Information Technology and Libraries*, **15** (1), 38–41.

JSTOR Journal Storage

http://www.jstor.ac.uk/

Law, D (1999) The organisation of collection management in academic libraries. In Jenkins, C and Morley, M (eds) *Collection management in academic libraries*, 2nd edn, Gower.

lis-medjournal-duplicates

http://www.mailbase.ac.uk/lists/lis-medjournal-duplicates/

NESLI model licence

http://www.nesli.ac.uk/nesli8a.html

OCLC FirstSearch Electronic Collections Online

http://www.oclc.org/oclc/menu/eco.htm

Smith, G (1999) The legal deposit of non-print publications: the 1998 Working Party on legal deposit, *Serials*, **12** (2), 125–9.

Smith, M (1998) Hanging on to what we've got: economic and management issues in providing perpetual access in an electronic environment, *Serials*, **11** (2), 133–41.

Standing Conference of National and University Libraries (1999) *SCONUL R Doc.99.91 Definitions and response sheets. Section 2: Provision of stock.*

Woodward, H (1999) Management of printed and electronic serials. In Jenkins, C and Morley, M (eds) *Collection management in academic libraries*, 2nd edn, Gower.

8

Exploitation and usage analysis

Roger Brown

Introduction

Two main areas will be covered in this chapter:

- exploiting the serials collections
- gathering usage data to aid collection management.

Most of the experiences and examples in this chapter will be drawn from the industrial sector, looking at workplace libraries and information services, though many of the comments, perhaps with some adjustment for particular situations, will also be applicable and relevant to libraries in other sectors. To give a little background on the author's workplace, SmithKline Beecham (SB) is a global healthcare company with offices in most countries of the world. SB Pharmaceuticals Research and Development is primarily located at sites in the UK and the USA. The Information Service in SB Pharmaceuticals Research and Development also operates globally, with networked services and intranets providing services to SB customers worldwide.

The term 'customer' is now widespread throughout this sector. This can be taken as synonymous with reader, patron or any other description for the users of the service, but does imply that the librarian as 'service provider' is accountable to the 'customer' for the delivery of an effective, value for money service.

Exploiting the serials collections

Some of the preceding chapters in this handbook have described how to select, acquire and display serials in your library. Much time and effort has been invested in achieving this, and the process has probably committed more of the library budget than any other heading apart from staff costs. So how do you ensure that your institution gets maximum value from, and return on, that investment?

This is where there are some differences in the type of library. In the corporate library every item has to pay its way. The collections are usually quite dynamic with a high rate of title turnover annually. The SB libraries' percentage turnover in 1999 was 8%. Academic libraries have traditionally been more stable, with emphasis on building collections for present and future research. But even that model is now changing, with budgetary shortfalls, challenges of electronic access, and academics and students, perhaps being based off-campus (even in different countries). These factors are contributing towards a more 'commercial' view on serial collections even for academic libraries.

What methods can be used to exploit the journal collections? The simplest can still be among the most effective.

Awareness

1 Printed lists of titles, depending on the size of the collection, either alphabetically or broken down by subject, can be useful to have available as handouts in the library or to accompany other promotion efforts.

2 A list of the changes for that year with new titles and cancellations will be useful for those customers who know the collections well, or for other library staff's awareness. This can also be produced in poster format for display around the library, especially the journal display area, or in customer departments.

3 The library catalogue or OPAC should also carry a statement of the current journal holdings.

4 The library web pages are another location for lists of current titles and holdings, though in this case there is more scope for enhancing the level of this information. In addition to the regular listing by title and by subject, it is increasingly important to note the format of the journal, in particular those that are available to customers electronically as well as in paper. A graphical symbol denoting paper, electronic (table of contents), electronic (abstracts) or electronic (full text), is a simple but effective method of indicating format.

5 The exploitation of the serials collection will be enhanced by the current awareness services that your institution uses to bring current information to your customers' attention. There is not the space here to cover these in depth, but services such as those provided by ingenta's BIDS *AutoJournals*, ISI's *Corporate Alert* (for tables of contents) or *Discovery Agent* (for personal profiles), *MEDLINE* or *SwetScan* will alert customers to table of contents of favourite journals as they appear, and/or relevant journal articles, select-

ed by the application of sometimes quite complicated search statements combining keywords through Boolean operators. These alerts may be presented in such a way that they can then be transferred by the customer directly into the library request system, or stored in one of the bibliographic management tools such as *Reference Manager* or *EndNote*. Electronic table of contents notification is now also offered without charge by many publishers from their websites, whether or not an individual or an institution subscribes to a particular title.

Marketing and promotion

The foregoing methods are simple and straightforward, but may miss the target audience completely. What about more innovative ways of reaching them? Remember that they are being bombarded by a plethora of other information. How are you going to get them to see and read yours? We know from studies in SmithKline Beecham that customers rarely read posters or notices, and unless the message is targeted at them, showing them how they will benefit personally from a piece of information, they will ignore it. So think laterally, be unconventional and experiment. It will take time and resources, but the end result will be that awareness (and hopefully use of) the journal collections will be better, and customers will feel that they are involved and a partner in the development of the journal collections, rather than just passive users. An additional spin-off benefit will be that management, and perhaps more importantly the top institution level management, will see the promotional efforts and will recognize the efforts being made to customize the collections to the institution's needs. This will do no harm at all when budget allocation time comes around.

These are some of the methods that could be tried:

1 Send targeted e-mails to Heads of Departments, academic/research groups, known information 'gatekeepers', and other individuals who have expressed an interest in the collections in the past. Remember the aim is to demonstrate how the library collections can personally benefit them.
2 Open houses, or 'journal days' could also be considered within the library. Use these as opportunities to collect feedback on any aspect of the collections be they paper or electronic. Take-up may be dependent on the nature of the institution, but as long as the potential visitors see some personal benefit in attending, bribed with coffee and cakes if necessary, some useful insights into the collections will be gained.
3 Attending customer department meetings is another option. Sometimes the invitation will come from the customer, but more likely expect to have to

engineer this, with the potential benefits to them explained upfront. The meetings might be team or department meetings at coffee or lunchtimes, or a special session in one of their own department meeting rooms. The promotion of electronic journals in SmithKline Beecham used department meetings as one of the publicity methods with excellent results.

4   Library web pages are a good vehicle to carry information on the journal collections. Make sure that there are links to the library pages from other relevant web pages in the institution. Wherever customers may need to check the collections is a good place to place a link, from, for example, the requesting system, from an internal bibliographic search service, or from the customer's department home pages.

5   Make sure that the library is represented in any induction/new employee orientation programmes. If the library is not responsible for these, or the library is not included in the programme directly, then it is even more important that something is provided in the new starter pack. But there will be far more information than the new employee can possibly assimilate. So keep it simple. Perhaps even to the extent of just a single brightly coloured page either inviting them to an informal orientation session, or pointing them to the library's web page address, where you will have a similar invitation to new starters highlighted on your home page.

Marketing and promotion checklist

- Send targeted e-mails to key customers.
- Hold journal 'open houses' or 'journal days'.
- Attend customers' internal meetings to promote the collections.
- Create links from any other web pages to the library collection web pages.
- Participate in new employee orientation programmes.

Usage analysis

The previous sections have been concerned with suggestions of how to reach your customers and raise their awareness of what is in the serials collection. The next step is to measure the actual use of those collections. The reasons for doing this include:

1   To help with decisions about which current journal subscriptions to take, including which journals to cancel should budgets demand this.

2   To assess the value of maintaining backfiles of certain journals. There is no value in storing back issues of titles that are no longer in demand, assuming

there are no archival responsibilities for those titles. Use that space to store current in-demand material.

3   To ensure that the library collections are aligned with the needs and objectives of the institution.

4   Lastly, usage figures will give important feedback information on the success, or otherwise, of the promotional activities that were intended to increase awareness and use of the collections.

Without this data, future purchase and holdings strategies will be based on perception and opinion rather than hard data. Collecting usage data is not easy, and has been challenging librarians for years. Herzog (1994) and Dole and Chang (1996) give examples of some of the possibilities. Briefly these are:

- counting the issues reshelved
- asking customers to sign a sheet either attached to the issue, or on a nearby shelf when they use an issue
- removing material from the active collection and seeing if anyone asks for it
- sealing the edge of issues with removable tape to see if anyone uses them
- analysing the loans or circulation data.

Counting items reshelved can include the issues returned from loan and those used by library staff for document delivery requests, as well as those left around the library by customers. In fact it may be breaking some customers' good habits by asking them not to reshelve the journals they have used. Other libraries never ask customers to reshelve used materials, expecting that they will put them back in the wrong place. It may only be necessary to count the reshelves of the most recently received material. But if every reshelve is recorded then it will be necessary to log the volume or issue year, or band of years. Titles change in prominence and importance over time, and some will have good usage from many years ago but little use currently (and vice versa). If you do not distinguish between these, you may arrive at a false conclusion about the need for the current subscription. But if space is an issue for your library, you may be able to show a usage pattern that will help determine your holdings policy for that title.

Attaching survey sheets to issues or shelves is a poor method of assessing real use, but when used in combination with the other methods described here could be useful. Some customers will not notice the survey sheets, some will see them but not fill them in, some might fill them in the first time but not when they subsequently use that title, and there is always the possibility that a customer will realize what is going on and attempt to overstate the use they make of a favourite journal, to improve the chances of the library keeping that title. It is also necessary to take into account the frequency of the title. Weeklies are bound to get more 'marks' than a monthly or quarterly. In fact if the survey only runs for a month or two, some quarterlies may be missed altogether. If during the survey period, a special issue featuring a particular topic is published, that should also be noted, since this may not be relevant to the customers' interest areas and be under-represented in your surveys, when other issues in the year may be very relevant.

Removing items from the collection and seeing if anyone asks for them could be used selectively. It is hardly appropriate for long backruns of journals, and is an unreliable method, since many customers will not ask at the reference desk for access to this material, they will simply go without – but would be most vociferous if the volumes were to be permanently removed.

Sealing issues with tape is not something that SmithKline Beecham has tried! Some customers may be reluctant to break the seal, so this is not a fool-proof method. At best it will indicate that the issue was used once, and one use per issue may not be a sound basis for keeping a title in the collection.

Analysing the loans data is only possible, of course, if journals are circulated or loaned, and many libraries do not offer this service. But, unlike some of the other methods described here, the analysis of such data will at least give a reasonably accurate indication of customer usage figures. As with the reshelving method, data collection by year is necessary to check that the current issues are in demand, if purchase decisions will be made on the basis of this analysis. If journal issues are circulated or routed, then the number of customers seeing each title could be factored into the data collection.

Ideally more information than this is needed if future subscription purchase decisions and journal collection management strategies are going to be made based on this data. Use every possible opportunity to gather comments, views and opinions. Ask for comments on the journal collections during formal or informal meetings with customers, even if that is not the main topic of the discussions. Customers will often mention something in passing that they would perhaps not raise more formally or officially, and this will give an early alert to potential problems or issues surrounding the collections.

Remember to consult other library staff, especially those on the enquiry/reference desk and those handling document delivery/interlibrary loans (ILL). They will know what titles customers are asking for, and have a pretty good idea as to what is being used within the library. Titles featuring strongly on ILL lists are good candidates for subscriptions, provided that it is recent volumes that are most popular, that there is evidence of sustained use over more than one year, and that the cost/benefit ratio is appropriate. For titles with a high annual subscription, continued reliance on ILLs, or some form of electronic document delivery, may be the most cost-effective option, even when there are a substantial number of requests each year.

Customer journal surveys

But there will still be a need in most institutions for a more structured systematic review of the journal collections (Bensman and Wilder, 1998). Probably the most common method of collecting customer feedback is by way of journal surveys. At SmithKline Beecham there is an annual survey, since the rate of title change is rapid, responding to changing research needs. Not all libraries need, or are able, to do surveys this frequently. Where there is relative stability in customers' information needs, a survey every three years may be sufficient.

Timing is critical to ensure good participation levels from customers in time to make subscription decisions ahead of the next subscription year. University libraries need to plan the timetable to avoid the summer examination period and then the start of the autumn term. This effectively means that the survey needs to be planned to start in the Christmas term for completion by Easter, for orders to be placed in August for the following year. So in this situation customers are surveyed a full 12 months before they see the outcomes of the survey reflected in the library collections. Commercial libraries need to react faster than that, and will try to survey as late as possible without jeopardizing the renewals process. The survey might be carried out in early/mid-summer with subscription decisions being made by August for order placement in September.

Journal surveys (or 'cancellation exercises' as some university libraries seem to call them) take many forms. But before the planning commences, it is important to set out the objectives and required outcomes. What is the primary objective? To show which current journals should be taken, or to help with back-holdings policy? To get feedback on what formats are important to customers? Or is it to enable the budget to be balanced? The construction of the survey will be different according to the importance of each of these objectives, so be sure of priorities at the outset.

Traditionally the journal survey is paper-based with lists of current subscriptions being circulated to key customer groups or their managers. They are asked to indicate which titles they regard as essential to hold in the library collection, and which other non-subscribed titles the library should also take. It is best to ask which journals researchers actually *use*, rather than which titles they feel should be bought. Even then, such lists can contain strange anomalies, including titles which cannot be traced at all, titles listed under a former name changed several years previously, titles that ceased publication some time ago, and titles cancelled by the library without any evidence of subsequent document delivery requests. Having ironed out such irregularities, this feedback is then processed, resulting in a ranked list of titles to which the institution should subscribe, and a second list of suggested additional titles.

There are many variations around this theme. Give customer groups an amount of the library budget to spend and leave them to decide which titles they take, give them a number of 'votes' to cast for specific titles (eg if each person has one hundred votes, they can give all hundred votes to one title, or one vote to one hundred different titles, or any combination in between), or ask customers to rank titles by importance eg essential, very useful, of interest, of no interest.

It is now possible to use web-based surveys rather than paper-based surveys. This has many advantages. The survey can be launched on the intranet to the whole institution simultaneously. Anyone who has an interest in the library collections can respond, rather than just those, usually senior, people who previously received the paper surveys, and may not have been the heaviest users of the library.

SmithKline Beecham's experience with web surveys is very good, with excellent response rates. It is now simpler for the customer since all they have to do, after they have told us who they are, is to click the titles they would like the library to subscribe to, and in what format they would like to see those titles – paper, electronic or both. The feedback can also be manipulated automatically to produce an analysis of the most requested titles.

If the library provides a document delivery service, then data from this can be added to the journals survey data. This may help support a customer's request for an additional title, if document delivery shows that it has been in demand recently. It may also show up titles that are held on-site but are requested from external suppliers. This may indicate a breakdown in the subscription system or some internal processing problem.

If a copy service from journals held on-site is provided, and demand is heavy for titles that customers have also asked to be held in the collection, then that will help support their case. But if customers are asking for titles that have low document delivery demand, then these need to be investigated.

If external data is needed on the citation level of journals in the collection then ISI (the Institute for Scientific Information) publish *Journal citation reports*, which include the journal impact factors. These give good information relating to the number of times other authors cite papers in particular journals, but this may not equate to usefulness in your own institution. Special care should be taken to compare impact factors for journals in cognate subject areas. Even the most essential engineering or veterinary journals will have impact factors much lower than relatively low-ranking journals in many biomedical fields.

Once the design and procedures are done the first time, it is simple to update the title lists and be ready for next year's survey. But whatever method used, there is one inevitable outcome: the available budget will not be enough to subscribe to all the titles customers request. So there follows a period of negotiation with customers to try to reach an acceptable solution. This takes time, and may result in customer groups feeling that they are the ones to have suffered at the expense of others, regardless of how fairly you try and share out the available resources.

Usage data collection checklist

- Count items reshelved.
- Attach survey sheets to journals.
- Restrict access by removing from active collections or sealing with tape.
- Analyse loans data.
- Gather information informally from customers and library staff.
- Carry out journal surveys.

Electronic usage measurement

The methods outlined in the previous section are all possible, but at best will give you relative qualitative rather than absolute quantitative data. The underlying difficulty is that all these methods result in customers listing their favourite journals, rather than the journals that they use and that give them the most value. That is simply human nature. But is there anything that can be done to improve the survey methods to get more accurate usage data?

Already the development of the electronic journal is promising much better usage data than we have ever had with paper journals. For the first time it should be possible to tell with certainty how many customers use 'Journal X', and to what level of detail. Do they view the contents pages? Do they view the abstract? Do they download a PDF file? How many PDF files from one issue do they download? Are there licensed titles that are not used at all?

Potentially, every action carried out by the customer can be tracked either by the library directly on its intranet, or from data supplied by the publisher/intermediary on the institution's use of their services. There will be no dispute as to the volume of use of a particular title. In a situation where a licensed title may not be held in the library in paper copy at all, then the usage data on the electronic version will be totally accurate, there being no other way for the customer to access it.

If an aggregator's services are used, then usage reports should be part of the package. If the institution has agreements with individual publishers, then the contract should stipulate the delivery of regular usage reports, at a level of detail agreed with the licensee. Not all publishers are yet technically able, or perhaps willing, to provide such usage data. But the contract should state that this is an expectation and set some timescale for their future provision.

Where such usage data is available, what should the library request or expect from the provider? There is not the space here to go into great detail, but the guidelines produced by the International Coalition of Library Consortia (ICOLC, 1998) are recommended reading. Downloads of full articles are an indication of more intensive use (although even then there is no guarantee that the article is actually *read*: we are all familiar with the notion that the act of photocopying or printing an article somehow causes the content to be transferred to the brain of the person receiving the copy). On the other hand, the number of hits on tables of contents pages, and abstracts, are also useful in revealing browsing activity.

There are also some technical issues here that may cause problems. For example, if the institution's server caches data, then the report from the publisher will not reflect true usage data, since some customer requests may be satisfied from the cache rather than the publisher's server. Another potential difficulty arises if the customer accesses the service from home or from another location away from the licensee's site, or if dynamic IP address are used (as is the case in many corporations), then the publisher may have difficulty identifying that customer as one of the licensee's group, and the usage reports may be incomplete as a result.

It is also the case that some publishers view this data as business confidential and are not willing to divulge any usage data. Less extreme, but also of concern, are those publishers that provide only partial information, for example just the top ten most used titles. The publishers' reluctance to provide detailed usage data may be based on the fear that it might show such a low level of usage that the subscriber then considers cancelling certain titles. But all the indications so far point to the opposite; that usage levels are higher than expected (Hirshon, 1999). The challenge then for the library is how to provide customers with access to the titles most in demand whilst maintaining budgetary control. However, this is what libraries have always done in the print-only environment. The additional benefit that web usage data brings is that for the first time the library can provide evidence of actual usage levels to the institution. If this can be combined with an analysis of the benefit such access brings, then there is a very sound basis for an application for additional funding. In the commercial environment, although funding is tight and closely controlled, a case for additional funding for services that bring value to the organization may sometimes be successful.

The fully virtual library should have no difficulty selecting the titles it wishes to have licensed access to, because it will know from the web statistics which titles are the most heavily used. That has many implications for libraries and for publishers (Brown, 1999), discussed above and in other chapters of this book, and will undoubtedly exercise others over the coming years. Nevertheless, the most likely scenario over the next few years is that it will still be necessary to try to measure use of print copies as well. Libraries will be hybrids of paper and electronic with many electronic titles remaining, in addition, as print subscriptions, while other journals – mainly outside the science/technology/medicine arena – will not yet have an electronic version.

Conclusion

As financial pressures grow, it becomes ever more important both to encourage as much use of the journal literature as possible through exploitation of existing collections and access to articles by means of document delivery; and to be able to measure use, in order to justify the considerable expenditure on serials. This chapter has discussed appropriate procedures, and promoted the role of the proactive serials manager in these essential activities.

References

AutoJournals
> http://www.bids.ac.uk/news/autojnls.html

Bensman, S J and Wilder, S J (1998) Scientific and technical serials holdings optimization in an inefficient market: a LSU serials redesign project exercise, *Library Resources and Technical Services*, **42** (3), 147–242.

Brown, R (1999) What happens next? E-journals in the corporate information service, *Serials*, **12** (2), 149–52.

Dole, W and Chang, S (1996) Survey and analysis of demand for journals at the State University of New York, *Library Acquisitions: Practice and Theory*, **20** (1), 23–38.

EndNote
> http://www.isinet.com/products/refman.html#endnote

Herzog, K (1994) Designing effective journal use studies, *Serials Librarian*, **24** (3/4), 189–92.

Hirshon, A (1999) Use levels and new models for consortial purchasing of electronic journals, *Library Consortium Management*, **1** (3/4), 47–58.

International Coalition of Library Consortia (1998) *Guidelines for statistical measures of usage of web-based indexed, abstracted and full text resources*, available at:
> http://www.library.yale.edu/consortia/webstats.html

ISI Corporate Alert
> http://www.isinet.com/products/ias/ca.html

ISI Discovery Agent
> http://www.isinet.com/products/ias/da.html

Reference Manager
   http://www.isinet.com/products/refman.html#refman
SwetScan
   http://www.swets.co.uk/sscan96.html

9

Signposts to the future

Martin White

A view from Signal Point

At the end of a book of such erudition I have found providing this personal
postscript on the future of serials management a daunting challenge, and this
chapter should be regarded more as an essay than as a detailed summary. The
text is based on a presentation I gave to the Chemical Information Group of the
Royal Society of Chemistry in early 1999. Later in 1999 I was invited to give a
paper on the future of scholarly communication to the Annual Meeting of the
Canadian Association of Research Libraries, which was held in St John's,
Newfoundland. From my hotel room I could see a building high on Signal
Point, a promontory overlooking the Atlantic Ocean, which marked the spot
where in December 1901 Marconi had first transmitted a radio signal across the
Atlantic to Poldu Cove in Cornwall. The Atlantic had first been spanned by
telegraph cable nearly 50 years earlier, but to me it was the invention of wireless that catalysed the remarkable rate of change in society and commerce that
we have witnessed over the last century.

Until quite recently the rate of change in scholarly communication has been
somewhat less rapid. As discussed in Chapter 1, the primary journal dates from
the 17th century, with the *Philosophical Transactions of the Royal Society* and the
French *Journal des Sçavans*, and the learned society publishing model that was
created continued largely unchanged until the period after World War 2. It was
the Royal Society that again provided the stimulus for change in its 1948
Conference on Scientific Information. Here for probably the first time scientists
started to address the issues of how the communication of scientific progress
was to be accomplished in a way that would match the inevitable growth in
scientific research in the post-war era. This is not the place for a detailed
critique of this conference, which was well reviewed in a special issue of the
Journal of Documentation (Line, 1998), but we can point out that between 1948
and 1998 there was in fact relatively little progress in developing new models of
scholarly communication, other than attempts to cope with the issues arising

from the invention of the photocopier. A notable exception was the arrival of commercial STM (science/technology/medicine) publishing houses, notably Pergamon and North Holland, and it is regrettable that the subsequent furore over the activities of Robert Maxwell has tended to diminish the rôle that he played in creating new STM publishing models.

In the 1980s there was no doubt that STM publishing became a very profitable business, but towards the end of the decade there were the first signs of concern that the combination of increases in the cost of subscriptions, and the number of new titles being published, were starting to get uncomfortably close to budget ceilings. Then came the UK Follett Report (Joint Funding Councils' Libraries Review Group, 1993), which will probably be seen as one of the fundamental agents of change in STM publishing, at least in the UK. One of the main objectives of this report was to look at the current and future impact of information technology on the provision of information. The report was one of the first systematic attempts to highlight the concern of many in the UK academic library community that the rate of increase in the cost of subscriptions to STM journals was outstripping the budget available to purchase these journals. The result was inevitably that journals were being cancelled, with implications for research, education and, of course, the publishing industry.

At roughly the same time Tim Berners-Lee was also looking at solutions to the issues of scholarly communication, and creating the building blocks of the world wide web. Of course some sections of academic and defence research had been using the Internet for some time, but the technical problems were quite substantial. The development of the web architecture addressed these problems quite brilliantly, and the natural desire of scientists to communicate did the rest (Berners-Lee, 1999).

At the outset in 1995 of the Pilot Site Licence Initiative (PSLI), funded by the UK's Higher Education Funding Councils with the main aim of reducing the cost of access to printed journals, the idea that electronic delivery of journals would be an important feature was not widely appreciated, and there was indeed little reason why this should be so. I was a member of the evaluation team for the PSLI, and in the course of my work in 1996/97 I visited most of the leading STM publishers. Several told me that they had no intention of joining the electronic world. Within less than a year all had made a major commitment to electronic delivery (White, 1997).

We are now at the stage that Marconi was at in 1901. We know that the technology works, though no doubt there will be enhancements to come. In 1901 there were others who were also very interested in what Marconi had accomplished. They were the cable companies, most of whom had brought their undersea cables ashore in Porthcurno, a few miles north of Poldhu Cove in Cornwall. As Marconi was transmitting the three dots of the letter S in morse code the head office of the Eastern Telegraph Company instructed the staff at Porthcurno to assess the impact of this technology. They reported that it had limitations, and was unlikely to take over from the established cable services in the near future. Within two decades wireless advanced to the extent that the British government realized that it made sense to integrate the companies providing the cable and wireless services, and Cable and Wireless Ltd was created.

There is a metaphor here for STM publishing. Electronic journals are still in their infancy, and still require special skills to get the best out of them. Print journals are much easier to manage. The future lies in the successful integration of the two. There are many forecasts of the imminent demise of print journals, but I think that the attributes of print will result in a coexistence, albeit not a very happy commercial one, for some years.

In this chapter I propose to look at the links in the chain of scholarly communication, and see which of the participants at the supply end of the complex chain will benefit or be placed at a disadvantage in the future, and where the opportunities lie for established and new providers of STM information.

Authors

The fundamental requirements of the author have been summarized so well by Karen Hunter of Elsevier that it is better that I quote her directly than try to paraphrase.

> Academic science researchers publish to establish their claim at a specific time to a specific result. They publish to gain other forms of recognition (such as promotion and tenure) that require publication. They publish in order to have independent certification of the results and to have those certified (refereed) results archived in perpetuity. Finally, they publish to communicate with those who may be interested in their works today – not the circle of cognoscenti (who do not need publication to be informed) but researchers in related fields, researchers in less well-connected institutions, and students working their way into the inner ring. (Hunter, 1998)

In respect of these requirements there is little real advantage to making an electronic version of the printed article available. Authors are often dismayed by how long it takes to get a paper published, but there have been well-established quick publication routes available for many years. In fact there seem to be more issues of concern than there are of benefit. Almost certainly there are going to be fewer subscriptions as consortia purchasing and cut-backs in other sectors reduce the number of individual subscriptions, though it may be that through campus networking more readers can gain access to the paper. The issue of archival access is going to come up a number of times in this discussion, and where an institution only has the electronic version, the extent to which the paper remains accessible to other researchers for perpetuity when the institution ceases the subscription is going to make for some interesting discussions. Where publication takes place in an electronic only format, and a number of such journals are now emerging, it also remains to be seen how these titles are assessed by those who have responsibility for the administration of research grants and the award of tenured positions.

This brings me to the subject of peer review, which during 1998 and 1999 has been a topic of intense discussion, largely through the success of the Los Alamos preprint server and the potential extension of the concept to biomedicine (Roberts, 1999). I am not going to come down on one side or the other in the debate, but to observe that there is a wide spectrum of opinion and there is little in the way of a consensus emerging. The speed of progress is quite stunning. The National Institutes of Health's newborn PubMed Central service has been raised in Chapters 2 and 3, but, although its future is by no means certain, it has moved very quickly in the last few months from an idea to something with widespread support (and scepticism) and a definite start date.

In the final analysis authors do want their papers to be read, and here the transaction log for a journal can be a two-edged sword. In the past, about the only external measure of usage has been through the ISI citation indexes. Publishers obviously have records of sales, but not of the readership of individual papers, or special issues. Librarians have always had to guess at readership, and ironically have more idea about the use made of titles they do not hold through ILL records than they do of their actual holdings. Librarians now wish to have records from publishers of the use made of titles, and the level of detail required, as set out in some guidelines published by the International Coalition of Library Consortia (ICOLC, 1998), seems to me not to be founded in reality. In the context of the author, the tracking of readership (or at least downloading) may reveal that no one is interested in the paper, and lead in time to the author finding it difficult to get published at all.

Enhanced functionality

The real benefits to the author are not likely to come until the electronic journal offers enhanced functionality to include a wide range of additional material which it would have been impossible to incorporate in a printed article. A recent survey of the current range of additional content has been undertaken (McKiernan, 1999), and this content is clearly going to grow in the near future. Examples include access to detailed spectra, and the ability to rotate and transform chemical structures, and to download additional data sets that cannot be cost-effectively included in the printed copy. Colour images are another example where the cost of providing these in an electronic journal is almost certainly cheaper than the cost of printing the images.

The academics who will be able to make use of these options are not primarily the senior staff and researchers, but will be the current generation of new graduates, to whom the computer desktop is their only desktop. In looking at the rate of development and use of electronic journals it is easy to see the issues and problems in terms of our own ability to use a PC, and to envision the future in those terms. We usually forget that others, younger than ourselves, have a different set of skills and objectives, and that we have to start to pay special attention to their requirements, or recognize that they have the technical skills to find alternatives.

Publishers

However you do the mathematics – there is little doubt that some STM publishers are adept at the mathematics of profit concealment – STM publishing has been an immensely profitable business for quite a number of publishers for many years. For example, in July 1999 it was announced that £60 million from the cumulated assets of the Oxford University Press were to be used to fund significant new developments at the University. Now publishers are facing a much more uncertain future in which many academics and librarians are asking how publishers can justify these profit margins, and also asking publishers to invest heavily in electronic journals.

Whenever two or more librarians gather together the topic of conversation usually gets round to 'Why don't publishers do A (and/or B and/or C)?' as though there was a stereotypical publisher. There is no such thing, and that has made the discussions between librarians and publishers, and even between publishers themselves, quite strained.

There are five main categories of STM publisher:

- the commercial 'for-profit' publishing companies, which include Elsevier, Wiley, Taylor & Francis, Academic Press, etc
- university presses, with many of the US presses being very notable innovators in publishing, such as Project Muse at Johns Hopkins and HighWire Press at Stanford University
- large professional societies with significant publishing operations, such as the American Chemical Society and the Institution of Electrical Engineers
- smaller professional societies, where publishing is one of the key member benefits, though the publishing activities may be outsourced to a commercial publisher

- a large number of special cases, such as *Nature* and the *New England Journal of Medicine*.

In total there are probably in excess of 15,000 publishers of serials, of which maybe only 1% have publishing revenues in excess of $1million. It is therefore very difficult, and indeed dangerous, to make sweeping statements about 'publishers' and their rôle in the development of electronic journals.

At present publishers are seen by authors, librarians, subscription agents and readers to be trying to preserve the status quo, and their profit margins. In defence of publishers few of the above (with the possible exception of subscription agents) have any idea of the level of investment required in terms of cash and staff to be an STM publisher. One of the few benefits is the positive cashflow that comes from the subscription model. Launching a new journal is always a long-term investment, and the adaptation of existing production processes to provide electronic journals is far from straightforward. Publishers are also having to invest in significantly larger sales and marketing teams, with legal support, to be able to negotiate the complex agreements that are now a major component of consortia purchasing.

Publishers are also having to come to terms with the fact that brand name means little in electronic delivery. It actually meant relatively little in print publishing, but the evidence from the market is that users like to have access to a cluster of journals that meet the majority of their needs, and have little interest in who is the publisher of the title. In any given discipline there will be a wide range of publishers, and users do not want to have multiple passwords and differing access protocols and search commands.

Just at the present moment life is pretty difficult for publishers. They are also facing demands to provide archives at no extra cost (even though this was not a service that they provided in the past) and also detailed logs of title usage, which again in the past was not their rôle. In the academic market consortia purchasing is now fast becoming the norm, and in the corporate market the requirement for delivery to a global intranet at a predetermined price is causing some very difficult problems in terms of pricing models. Add to that the restructuring (a nice word for 'acquisition') in the pharmaceutical industry, and a whole host of new 'publishing' initiatives such as SPARC, and I think you will see that life as a publisher is just a little difficult.

Technological opportunities

The new technology should, however, bring many opportunities to the publisher who is able to think more creatively. The future lies in gaining a substantially better understanding of the requirements of users, something that neither the librarian nor the publisher were concerned about in the past, mainly because there was little that could be done about finding out just what the requirements of users actually were. The advent of the logging of transactions from servers, together with an increasing (but still very inadequate) level of research into how users want to identify, access and use electronic journals, will lead to a range of electronic journal formats that take advantage of computer technology.

We tend to forget that we are still in the very infancy of electronic journals and that indeed there is very considerable scope for added content and functionality, as standards such as XML are adopted, and bandwidth increases to enable substantially larger files to be downloaded. There is also the option to move more material towards full-colour printing. This has always been expensive and time-consuming for publishers, but given the cost of colour printers this could be an important opportunity, especially in the fields of medicine and biochemistry.

Incidentally, I have no doubts that the format of the scientific paper will itself change. The current structure has suited the constraints of the printed page for several centuries, but is often inflexible. To me there is a good argument for looking at the structure of formal communication in science, perhaps along the line of the modular approach proposed by Kircz (1998) and Smith (1999), in which the traditional 'story telling' sequence of a paper, from abstract, through the introduction, objectives, methodology, results, conclusions and finally the bibliography, becomes something where individual sections can stand on their own. As the electronic functionality progresses, and the electronic format is able to diverge significantly from being the digital version of the printed format, publishers will be able to differentiate their titles in a way that has just not been possible up to now. The ease with which multimedia and additional files can be added to the paper will start to be an important factor for an author deciding where to publish.

Secondary services

Just where all these developments leave the secondary services is difficult to see at present. Certainly ISI has recognized the need for action in the development of the *Web of Science*, realizing that it is not sensible to provide a web-accessed version of the range of citation indexes, without rethinking the way in which researchers will want to use the databases in a web environment, for example with full-text links to journal articles (as are also being developed by other database providers).

One important rôle that the traditional abstracting and indexing services do need to fulfil is the linking of content from before the electronic age. Although there are some indications that the useful life of a scientific paper might only be five years, and that as the electronic archive develops the need to identify earlier research will diminish rapidly, I think this is a potentially dangerous assumption, and could lead at the very least to the duplication of research. Even in the age of electronic journals there will continue to be many titles that remain in a print only format, and these also need to be able to be identified. Interestingly over the last few years there have been many conferences, and even more papers, on the future of primary publishing, but very few indeed on the issues and opportunities for the secondary publishing industry.

One of these issues is the ownership of the metadata that is added to the paper by the primary publisher. In the past it was the secondary service that often rewrote the abstract in a consistent style and added indexing terms. Now that the original abstract is in an electronic format, enriched by metadata (hopefully), the business model that used to exist between the primary publisher and the secondary service is bound to change. The secondary service is also going to have to cope with finding a way to identify and index additional files that are associated with the paper.

Tertiary publishing

Although this chapter appears in a book on serials management it is important not to forget the rôle that review journals play in the identification of primary material, and also the use made of primary material in monographs. To date the focus of attention on just the primary publication of research is probably justified, but could ultimately lead to some significant problems in the future unless the entire panoply of scholarly communication is considered (Kircz, 1998). I also find the research being undertaken in the HERON project based at the University of Stirling of great interest, though I think it may be a little while before we can fully see where this initiative is going. The objectives of HERON are to develop a national database and resource bank of electronic texts which will widen access to course materials and improve the quality of learning throughout higher education in the UK; to collaborate with rights holders and representative bodies to remove blockages in copyright clearance and to determine appropriate fee levels and conditions for the digital age; and to offer opportunities to universities and colleges to market their own learning resources. The technology of e-books is also developing rapidly, and I am quite certain that over the next few years the tertiary business will go through a substantial period of change.

Subscription agents

For subscription agents the last few years have been challenging ones. The larger agents realize that there is an opportunity to provide services to their users which aggregate electronic titles from a number of different publishers under one interface. This has emerged as an important user requirement, especially if it facilitates access to a cluster of related journals from different publishers. In addition the provision of these services can lead to increased subscriber lock-in, and provide more scope to differentiate each agent from competitors at a time when existing service differentials had become almost minimal.

To undertake this rôle, the agents must make substantial investments in information systems and staff from a revenue stream which used to be margin-based through leveraging the discounts they negotiated from publishers. There are limits to this approach, and they were reached by Blackwell's Information Services in 1998 when the company lost over £5 million on a turnover of £250 million, compared with a small profit on virtually the same revenues in 1997. This information was not released until after the joint venture between Swets and Blackwell's Information Services was announced in June 1999. Later in 1999 RoweCom announced that it had acquired the subscription agency business of Dawsons. This leaves three very large global agents, Swets/Blackwells, RoweCom/Dawsons, and EBSCO/Lange & Springer, and a somewhat uncertain future for the many smaller agents, although there may well still be niche markets in which they can operate successfully.

As well as the complications of electronic journals the agents have also been coping with the problems associated with consortium acquisition, where in a given consortium there may be a number of different agents involved. This has produced complications in a number of situations where one agent was used for serials management, and another for book acquisition. In the corporate sector journal purchasers have often used a different agent in North America from that in Europe, and again this has led to long negotiations between agents and customers.

Librarians

A major stimulus to the current revolution in scholarly communication has been the result of actions taken by librarians to square the circle of the costs of acquiring serials against constraints of budgets, and started with the development of consortia purchasing, for example OhioLINK in the USA. In 1996/97 the requirement to control serials purchasing expenditure coincided with initiatives from a number of publishers, for example Elsevier, Institute of Physics

Publishing, Academic Press and the Association for Computing Machinery (ACM), to develop electronic versions of their print serials. The original pricing model often bundled in the electronic version at either no additional cost, or a small premium, on the print subscription. As a result many librarians and academics took the view that the costs of producing the electronic file were clearly so small that the costs of providing access to journals could be significantly reduced by subscribing to an electronic service, and taking perhaps just one copy of the paper version as an archive.

A number of problems arose from this somewhat simplistic view. The first was that the publishers could not play the game according to these rules. The cost of creating the initial file was probably as high as 70% of the total cost, and this was not going to reduce substantially in the near future. Secondly, subscription agents would also lose substantial income from this approach. The third problem, and one that is only now being fully recognized, is that the price of the product may have decreased (or at least not risen as quickly as before), but the additional systems management costs, and in particular the staff time and effort on managing these electronic services, were not fully appreciated (Duranceau, 1998).

There is no doubt that the original objective of the library community – to find a way to manage their serials budgets – was motivated by a need to maintain service levels to users. However, these service levels were based mainly on the number of titles held, rather than specific, quantifiable, levels of service.

User feedback

Of course all the members at the supply end of the communication chain have always paid lip service at least to the concept that their primary objective was the satisfaction of their users' needs. However, in a time of stable systems there was little impetus to question long-held assumptions about those needs. In my opinion, the many organizational problems associated with the management of serials in an electronic environment have obscured two very important developments.

The first is that, because the new age has brought problems to everyone, authors, publishers, subscription agents, librarians and users are beginning to realize how interdependent they all are. I have been quite amazed in the past by how little each group knew about the others, and as a result made demands on each other that were quite impracticable to achieve. There is still much to do in the areas of education and training, but at least the will is there.

The second is that there is now the communications infrastructure and incentive for a lively debate on the scholarly communication process, currently led in some style by Steven Harnad, at present Professor of Cognitive Science at the University of Southampton (Harnad, 1999). Harnad's views on scholarly communication, discussed elsewhere in this book, are controversial, but he deserves an accolade for his ability and readiness to comment in e-mail discussion lists and elsewhere, keeping pushing the debate onwards. The range of current initiatives is very broad, and well beyond the scope of this chapter to review, especially as without doubt over the next few years some of these will fall by the wayside, and new (or revised) ones will be promoted.

The challenge for the serials manager is to meet current user requirements in a way that does not prejudice the future, and that is a tall order, especially in an academic institution where the academic year cycle can be a significant constraint to service innovation.

In the UK we have been especially fortunate that the UK Serials Group has been able to act as a focus for this debate, and that the Higher Education Funding Councils had the vision to fund the PSLI, now developed into NESLI, from which many of the issues could be identified, though few solved. The eLib Programme has also been invaluable as a learning experience. It is gratifying to note the growth of serials groups throughout Europe, even when in many countries (Germany is one example) state-level budget management does mean that national initiatives are very difficult to fund and manage. In the USA the Association of Research Libraries has played a very important role, as has the work of Ann Okerson at Yale, for example, establishing the LIBLICENSE Project (Okerson, 1999).

In conclusion

I suppose my conclusion has to be that I have no conclusions. There is the much-quoted Chinese saying 'May you live in interesting times'. We certainly do at the present moment, with many challenges for all those involved in serials management, and in STM publishing. They are also sometimes frustrating times, as we try to cope with not one but apparently several paradigm shifts at the same time. All this is happening, against a background, for example, of proposed changes in intellectual property legislation in the European Union and the USA. The solution is always to stay close to our customers, whether they are paying us money, or using a service we provide. If we try to build better systems to replicate the present, the only certain outcome is that they will be outmoded before they can be effective. We have to be light on our feet, testing out possible approaches, working in partnership with everyone, and being receptive to new ideas and services.

Above all we must be ready to identify and exchange best practice, and this is what this book has illustrated. Tomorrow's best practice may be different, but for now what you have read in this book puts forward some of today's current thinking, and gives an invaluable base to build on for the future, which is, without doubt, going to be very interesting indeed.

References

Association of Research Libraries
   http://www.arl.org/
Bailey, C (ed) *Scholarly electronic publishing (bibliography)*, available at:
   http://info.lib.uh.edu/sepb/sepb.html
Berners-Lee, T (1999) *Weaving the Web*, Orion.
Duranceau, E F (1998) Beyond print: revisioning serials acquisitions for the digital
   age, *Serials Librarian*, **33** (1–2), 83–106, available at:
   http://web.mit.edu/waynej/www/duranceau.htm
eLib: the Electronic Libraries Programme
   http://www.ukoln.ac.uk/services/elib/
Harnad, S (1999) *Steven Harnad e-prints on interactive publication*, available at:
   http://cogsci.soton.ac.uk/~harnad/intpub.html
HERON: Higher Education Resources ON-demand
   http://www.stir.ac.uk/infoserv/heron/
Hunter, K (1998) Electronic journal publishing: observations from the inside, *D-Lib
   Magazine*, (July/August), available at
   http://mirrored.ukoln.ac.uk/lis-journals/dlib/dlib/dlib/july98/07hunter.html
International Coalition of Library Consortia (1998) *Guidelines for statistical measures
   of usage of web-based indexed, abstracted and full text resources*, available at:
   http://www.library.yale.edu/consortia/webstats.html
Joint Funding Councils' Libraries Review Group (1993) *Report* [The Follett Report],
   Higher Education Funding Council for England, available at:
   http://www.ukoln.ac.uk/services/papers/follett/report/
Kircz, J G (1998) Modularity: the next form of scientific information presentation,
   Journal of Documentation, **54** (2), 210–35.
Line, M (1998) An information world apart: the Royal Society Scientific Information
   Conference of 1948 in the light of 1998, *Journal of Documentation*, **54** (3), (June
   1998), 281–302.
M-Bed(sm): a registry of embedded multimedia electronic journals
   http://www.public.iastate.edu/~CYBERSTACKS/M-Bed.htm
McKiernan, G (1999) Embedded multimedia in electronic journals, *Multimedia
   Information and Technology*, **25** (4), 338–43.
Okerson, A (1999) The LIBLICENSE Project and how it grows, *D-Lib Magazine*, **5**
   (9), available at:
   http://www.dlib.org/dlib/september99/okerson/09okerson.html

Roberts, P (1999) Scholarly publishing, peer review and the Internet, *First Monday*, **4** (4), available at:
http://www.firstmonday.dk/issues/issue4_4/proberts/index.html

TFPL/Blackwell's guide to electronic journal management (1999), TFPL.

Smith, J W T (1999) The deconstructed journal – a new model for academic publishing, *Learned Publishing*, **12** (2), available at:
http://library.ukc.ac.uk/library/papers/jwts/d-journal.htm

White, M S (1997) From PSLI to NESLI: site licensing for electronic journals in UK academic institutions, *The New Review of Academic Librarianship*, **3**, 139–50.

Index